KASHMIR
as I see it

Praise For The Book

'Enjoyed reading the book as a personal memoir. The part about the author's childhood is very interesting. It will add to the existing literature on Kashmir.'

Krishnan Srinivasan,
Former Indian Foreign Secretary

'Rich in personal insights and intriguing anecdotes… Serious discussion on the internal politics of Kashmir and provides glimpses of particular events and turning points that are not widely known.'

Sumit Ganguly,
Professor, Indiana University, USA
Author, *The Crisis in Kashmir: Portents of War, Hopes of Peace*

'It is a product of hard work and embodies a lot of information both about the author and Kashmir. Such information is of vital significance in the present context of politics in India and Kashmir.'

Jayanta Bandyopadhyay,
Former Professor of IIM Calcutta, **India**

'Highly educative and enjoyable…'

Hari Vasudevan,
Former Professor of History,
University of Calcutta, India

'The uniqueness of the book lies in the manner in which the personal is juxtaposed with the political…it presents a deep understanding of Kashmiriyat and the essence of Kashmiri existence.'

Bandana Chatterji,
Sociologist, Kolkata, India

'A memoir which deftly deals with the long history, complicated present and possible future of Kashmir.'

Rakhahari Chatterji,
Former Dean of Arts,
University of Calcutta, India

KASHMIR
as I see it

FROM WITHIN AND AFAR

Ashok Dhar

RUPA

Published by
Rupa Publications India Pvt. Ltd 2019
7/16, Ansari Road, Daryaganj
New Delhi 110002

Sales Centres:
Allahabad Bengaluru Chennai
Hyderabad Jaipur Kathmandu
Kolkata Mumbai

ISBN: 978-93-5333-458-1

First impression 2019

10 9 8 7 6 5 4 2 3 1

The moral right of the author has been asserted.

In memory of my parents, Sheila and Soom Nath Dhar,
originally residents of Nai Sarak
and then 334 Jawahar Nagar, Srinagar, Kashmir.
In remembrance of their abiding faith in Kashmiriyat
till they breathed their last,
on 30 March 2010 in Mumbai
and on 1 January 2018 in Jammu, respectively.

CONTENTS

Foreword   *ix*

Introduction   *xiii*

My Kashmir

Growing Up   3

Origins and Early Inhabitants   14

Being Kashmiri   28

Uncontested Past   35

Mystery of the Holy Relic   43

Trust Me, Trust Me Not   50

Travelogue

Kashmir to Kumaon   65

Pakistan (Safar Apour)   70

Global Perceptions   85

The Misunderstood Maharaja   92

Sheikh Abdullah's Kashmir Saga   101

Simla Accord—The Real Story   114

My Destiny

Rebellious Decade   125

Convert, Leave or Die (Raliv, Tsaliv, Galiv)   137
Beyond Exodus and Backchannel Diplomacy   144
On the Top of the Day (Vaarai Chuss)   158
Multidimensional Dispute   166
Re-imagining the Vision   178

Appendix-1: Exodus of Kashmiri Pandits   201
Epilogue   207
Acknowledgements   210
Bibliography/References   213
Index   223

FOREWORD

T.S. Eliot once said, 'Home is where one starts from.' For Ashok Dhar, Kashmir is home because that is where he was born and schooled, and from where he set off into the wider world and had a career as an engineer and corporate executive specializing in energy. Meanwhile, that home devastated by an insurgency has had thousands dead and injured, tens of thousands displaced, and has opened psychological wounds that will take generations to heal.

Dhar, like many of his fellow Kashmiri Pandits, is unlikely to go back to Kashmir. But for him Kashmir will always be home. For this reason, it is difficult to classify the genre of the book because it is part autobiographical, part historical and part prescriptive. But all these parts come together when mixed with the key ingredients that have helped put it together—a burning passion for Kashmir and an overwhelming sense of sadness at the way things have changed.

There is something about Kashmir that excites imagination. Some of it has to do with its extraordinary physical beauty, but a great deal of it relates to its history and culture. Its recent history has not been too happy. The trauma that society has suffered makes many wonder whether its fabled culture, Kashmiriyat, has survived. Such a situation naturally breeds nostalgia and regret in equal measure. Dhar has now settled into the soothing environs of a think tank, the Observer Research Foundation (ORF) in Kolkata, and, perhaps because he is an engineer and a corporate man, his position on Kashmir does not come from any known ideological perspective. If anything, what stands out is his fervour for Kashmir and Kashmiriyat, and a desire to determine what went wrong and why, and how it can be set right.

He is no angry Pandit wanting retribution for his exile, but someone who has no hesitation in saying that mistrust between the people and the government has been a major reason for Kashmir to have been subjugated by others. And that, perhaps, Kashmiris must themselves take some blame for their current predicament.

Dhar's desire to delve into the past is not just about longing. Trained as an engineer, he inevitably breaks down the problem into its constituent parts and tries to reconstitute it into a workable solution. His effort has led him to study the history, culture and contemporary accounts related to Kashmir and mix them with his own memory of conversations, recollections and comments on the subject. He is quite forthright in stating that his goal is to initiate a conversation to define what could help restore some measure of normalcy to the state. But this is not just about solutions. Dhar's is also a deep meditation on who or what a Kashmiri is, their history and how they relate to one another—be they Muslim, Pandit or Sikh—interspersed with verses of Kashmiri poetry and song. A deep sense of spiritualism is evident in the account, born of the firm belief that that is the Kashmiri way.

A striking feature of Kashmir is its intellectual tradition born of the confluence of Shaivism, Buddhism and Islam. The more interesting element is the fact that all three have been deeply imbued with spiritualism, something that emerges sharply from Dhar's narrative.

Perhaps the most fascinating part of the book is the effort by Dhar to examine the various options for a resolution of the Kashmir situation. He has surveyed the existing literature that looks at different models—from the Trieste-Saar model to Ireland, Åaland and the Aceh Accord.

His conclusion is that one or more of these could be applied to Jammu and Kashmir (J&K), provided both India and Pakistan cooperate with each other in finding a solution. However, as of now, there seems little chance of that.

At the next level, he has sought to apply management decision-making tools to the problem—in particular, the Game Theory. To this end, he looks at various papers written on the issue and comes up with his own Dove-Hawk Game to see if there can be a way forward. After examining it, he thinks that changing the status quo is the most likely solution based on historical data, howsoever uncomfortable. However, to make it work, the two sides, India and Pakistan, need to work together to address the issues that could aid the process, such as legality, land, morality, operationality, Kashmiriyat, Sufism, historicity and identity (LeLaMOKSHI).

One thing is clear; the solution to the Kashmir issue will not come through the application of mathematical models and formulae. It will come through human agency, and will require courage and statesmanship of the kind that Jawaharlal Nehru displayed in 1947, or Atal Bihari Vajpayee in 2003, in understanding that the issue is not so much about legal rights and wrongs but about a human understanding of the fact that Kashmir is a unique problem requiring a unique solution, and that the Indian Constitution has enough room to provide it. Equally important is the need to understand that the government will need to reach out to Pakistan. The experience of 2004–2007, when back-channel talks almost resulted in working out a deal, signals that nothing is impossible. But what is important is that the domestic and external components of the solution be effectively synchronized. There is little point in making a breakthrough with Pakistan and forgetting the people in the state, or vice versa. If the true resolution of the Kashmir problem is subject to conditions that are difficult to meet today, the obvious option is to manage the situation to ensure that the violence and the tensions are kept to a minimum. Essentially, this was the strategy of the two countries when they began their composite dialogue, whose goal was to solve smaller problems like Siachen, Sir Creek and Wullar Barrage and build confidence towards resolving the larger issues of terrorism and Kashmir. Today, however, even composite dialogue appears to have reached a dead end.

This would suggest that the nightmare of Kashmir will carry on for some more time. Violence that had declined is now showing an uptick. Gunmen roam the land, and all it takes is one gunshot to disrupt peace. A sustainable solution to the Kashmir issue requires all three parties—New Delhi, Islamabad and Srinagar—to act in a synchronized manner towards broadly agreed objectives. This is an even taller order, requiring, as it does, not only a desire for a solution, but also statesmanship on the part of the leaders of both countries and the region of Kashmir.

Dr Manoj Joshi,
Distinguished Fellow & Head,
National Security Programme at the
Observer Research Foundation,
New Delhi

INTRODUCTION

What is in a name? A lot, if the name is Kashmir or 'Cashmere'.

Kashmir has been the subject of a lot of research; thousands of books have been written describing its beauty, people, culture and socio-economic dimensions. Kashmir's turbulent history, focussing on the post-1947 dispute between India and Pakistan over its accession to India, has given rise to an umpteen number of scholarly articles dealing with its problems and suggesting solutions for resolving disputes between the two countries.

South Asia has been witness to hostilities between India and Pakistan since India gained Independence in 1947 and Pakistan was born as a result of Partition. Since then, India and Pakistan have fought four wars in 1947, 1965, 1971 and 1999. Both are now nuclear states. Peace in the region has been threatened in the past seventy years chiefly due to the dispute over Kashmir. Resolution of the Kashmir dispute is, therefore, aimed at bringing peace and prosperity to the region.

Since I was born and brought up in Kashmir, I kept pace with contemporary events. As I go down memory lane to write a personal narrative, it is quite natural for me to reflect upon the background of the dispute and think about ways in which it can be resolved. If the beauty of Kashmir and some intriguing anecdotes have remained deeply etched in my memory, so has the urge to share my understanding and feelings with my dear fellow Kashmiris. Hopefully, it will interest people and policymakers in the subcontinent, and international players as well.

Having worked in the corporate sector in India and abroad and not being a research scholar, I am handicapped and cannot grasp the depth and breadth of commentaries made by so many writers and scholars about Kashmir. I keep wondering what should be done to have a peaceful, progressive and prosperous South Asia. So I began my journey of reading some scholarly works on Kashmir and drawing upon my experiences of life thus far.

Most people I spoke to and some political leaders hold the political leadership in Kashmir responsible for misleading the younger generation; they feel they have to respect their role and responsibility in the ongoing conflict. It is not uncommon to see politicians from Kashmir say something in Kashmir, something very different in Delhi and then something completely opposite in Islamabad.

Although the Kashmir conflict is seen primarily as a territorial one, I have often wondered whether that is the true nature of this long-standing dispute.

What about historicity, geography, leadership, and national and international players? Why don't we see Kashmir through these prisms as well?

My own understanding was enriched, thanks to a wealth of books on Kashmir, including Kalhana's *Rajatarangini*.[1] Ambassador Haqqani writes in his book, *Reimagining Pakistan*, that Pakistan no longer enjoys the support of the international community on the Kashmir issue. When former prime minister Nawaz Sharif raised the Kashmir issue in the United Nations

General Assembly (UNGA) in 2014, he was the only head of government to mention Kashmir out of 193 speakers. Yet leaders refuse to look beyond the Kashmir issue when talking about India-Pakistan relations. Ideology and pride come in the way of charting a sensible course.

Apart from the insight gained from these books, I also included recollections my upbringing in a Kashmiri family in the Valley, and interactions with friends, relatives, teachers and the society at large. I also recollected various conversations with people I have met during my employment and travels in India and abroad to help find answers independently to questions engaging my attention. The conversations as quoted in this book are what I remember to the best of my records, recollection and memory. I also recognize that writing about history and analysing historical events is a highly specialized work undertaken by historians and social scientists, and my personal limitations in this regard due to my background are plentiful. Whatever I have cited is my understanding, analysis and recollection of history and events while pursuing my early education in Kashmir, and later shaped by my reading books on the subject. I hope my observations and learning can help initiate a dialogue on what we want, what we have lost and what we can gain. I have tried to share my experiences in three parts.

Part I recounts my experiences from my years growing up in Kashmir and identifies the historical and cultural differences of Kashmir vis-à-vis the rest of India and other parts of the world as seen by me. It explains the historical development and contextualization of Kashmiriyat, Shaivism and Sufism. The objective of this part is to highlight some under-reported and lesser-known facts about the interrelation between Kashmiri culture and Lal Ded, a Kashmiri mystic living in the fourteenth century. It further dwells on areas that require a deeper understanding in terms of historicity, legality and morality.

Part II deals with my experience from travels to Islamic countries like Saudi Arabia, Iran and Pakistan, and captures the differences in the practice of Islam and Kashmiriyat in these countries and Kashmir. It also focusses on the role played by key personalities like Maharaja Hari Singh, Sheikh Mohammad Abdullah and Indira Gandhi in the post-1947 events in Kashmir, based on in-depth research.

Part III is a discussion and analysis of the 'Kashmir dispute' as a subject of Management, in corporate style, based on my experience of using tools like Game Theory and scenario-planning to suggest pathways for the future. This part is based on the analysis of various efforts (including back-channel diplomacy) to resolve the dispute in Kashmir, and uses social media as a source of input to assess the current feelings' of Kashmiris who are the *waadi ki awaz*, or the voice of the Valley. It also reviews solutions of similar disputes globally and their relevance to the current crises in Kashmir.

It is important for people in J&K and decision makers to know who we are and what we want to be. Piecemeal reactive solutions have been the past practice to addressing problems from crisis to crisis in the Valley. So stone throwers are answered by pellet guns, when law and order should be just an issue of local governance. A pragmatic solution must be holistic if it has to address any deep-set crisis afflicting a community. The book attempts to look at the issue expansively and suggest contours of pathways for a solution. Those who do not learn from history are condemned to repeat it.

Lastly, I wish to share with the readers of this book my pledge to contribute my royalty earnings from this book to philanthropic activities in Kashmir, which will, I hope, help in the revival of our synergetic culture.

PART I

MY KASHMIR

1

GROWING UP

When I was growing up in the early 1960s in Srinagar, I remember accompanying my father for the morning bath at the neighbouring ghat on the Jhelum (Vitasta) river, near the Ganpatyar temple. After a quick dip in the water, we would attend morning aarti prayers at the oldest temple of Lord Ganesha in Kashmir.

Just a hundred metres away was a mosque at Malyaar, visited by Muslims in the locality as it had a hammam bathhouse. Everyone longed for a free hot-water bath for warmth in the winters.

Even today I remember the soothing aarti at the temple (Om Jai Jagdish Hare) and the azan recital of the taqbir from the mosque. It was a common thing for Kashmiri Pandits (Hindus) and Muslims to meet at a shop serving halal meat after offering prayers. Such was our life while growing up in Kashmir, full of stories of religious tolerance and cultural amalgamation.[1]

In fact, the first word I ever spoke was from a lullaby sung into my ear by my maternal grandmother and mother.

Hukus bukus telli wann che kus,
Onum batta lodum deag,
Shaal kich kich waangano,
Brahmi charas puane chhokum
Brahmish batanye tekhis tyakha.

This was, and still is, the most popular lullaby in Kashmir. Years later, as I grew older, I learnt the correct version of the lullaby and realized how deeply it was rooted in Kashmir's spiritual tradition. The lullaby is ageless; while some believe it to be penned by Lal Ded, others ascribe its origin to the origin of Kashmir and Kashmiri culture. It continues to serve as a poetic medium to pass down Kashmiri culture and ethos from generation to generation. The song, which has a calming effect on all children in the lap of their mothers, has such depth that it may help people understand what separates Kashmir's culture from others. The actual song and its meaning is as follows:[2]

Tse kus be kus teli wan su kus
Moh batuk logum deg
Shwas khich khich wang–mayam
Bhruman daras poyun chokum
Tekis takya bane tyuk

[Who are you and who am I? Who is the creator that permeates both you and me?
Each day I feed my senses/body with the food of worldly attachment and material love (*moh*: attachment)
For when the breath that I take in reaches the point of complete purification (*shwas*: breath)
It feels like my mind is bathing in the water of divine love (*bhruman*: nerve centre in the human brain, *poyun*: water)

Then I know I am like that sandalwood which is pasted for divine fragrance symbolic of universal divinity. I realize that I am, indeed, divine. (*tyuk*: tika applied on the forehead)]

Hukus bukus or *Tse kus be kus*. Respect for universal divinity is a cultural ethos in Kashmir that begins very early in life for pursuing more spiritual than material goals. There is the belief that one is indeed divine, that the creator permeates all of us, that what feeds our senses or body is only attachments. Such thoughts of universal divinity are ingrained in Kashmiris when they are toddlers, and remain the connecting link for Kashmiris from generation to generation.

Memories of shikara rides on Dal Lake, trekking in the Zabarwan Hills, eating fresh fried trout in Pahalgam and visiting temples, Sufi shrines and dargahs often flash upon the inner eye. Three words also keep reminding me of a distinct identity—Kashmiriyat, Sufism and Kashmiri Shaivism. Kashmir is a land where three religions—Hinduism, Buddhism and Islam—have coexisted.

HISTORICITY IN KASHMIR

Kashmir has seen a number of Hindu, Mughal, Afghan, Sikh and Dogra rulers.[3] Till the death of Kota Rani in AD 1339, Kashmir was ruled by kings following Buddhist or Hindu/Vedic beliefs. The Muslim rule of the Shah Mir dynasty lasted until 1586, when the last Chak ruler surrendered to the Mughal emperor, Akbar. The Mughals governed Kashmir through various governors from AD 1587 to AD 1752. Then came the Afghans, who ruled from AD 1752 to AD 1819, the Sikhs from AD 1819 to AD 1846 and the Dogras from AD 1846 to AD 1947.

Kashmir was a Vedic society and Hinduism flourished for over a thousand years until Buddhism set down its roots there. Buddhism was brought to Kashmir by King Ashoka around the middle of the third century BC, but it received wider acceptance after Kanishka hosted the Fourth Buddhist Council at Kundalavana in Kashmir in AD 72. It was at this council that the Mahayana sect emerged as the superior of the two sects, Mahayana and Hinayana. Kanishka encouraged Buddhism and propagated the same within Kashmir and outside, to far-reaching regions. Buddhism prevailed from the third century BC to around the twelfth century. However, Buddhism suffered in popularity after the end of the rule of the Kushana dynasty and in the fifth century due to attacks by the Hun ruler, Mihirakula. By the time Adi Shankaracharya began the revival of Hinduism in the south and reached Kashmir, an enlightened version of Shaivite thought had given shape to Kashmiri Shaivism as propounded by Abhinavagupta.

Kashmiri Shaivism appealed to the masses and the reconversion of Buddhists to Hinduism began, possibly after the fifth century AD. Conversion from Hinduism to Buddhism was driven more by spiritual discourses rather than by any force or coercion. Both religions coexisted and neither made attempts to thwart the expansion of the other.

This was also when Lal Ded (1320–1392), the great Kashmiri mystic poetess, started explaining the essence of Kashmiri Shaivism in an easy-to-understand form of poetry, called Lal Vaakh ('vaakh' means language or sound while Lal means spoken by Lal Ded). She composed verses in the Kashmiri language. According to Dr George Grierson, Kashmiri language has a Dardic base, composed of various dialects spoken by the people in Kashmir, Ladakh, Baltistan and Dardistan.[4] The Kashmiri language existed much before the entry of the Sanskrit-speaking

Aryan settlers from Punjab and other parts of India.

A special feature of Kashmiri Shaivism (also known as Trika philosophy) is that it sees the 'Supreme unity of self with God'. One recognizes himself or herself as Shiva in a non-dualistic or monistic tradition. It gives primacy to 'universal consciousness' and sees all things as a manifestation of 'consciousness'. It believes that the world is real and existing, not an illusion (maya). It sees Lord Shiva as an actor (nartaka) who projects the drama on the screen, which is the world. Shiva is seen as the entirety of the universe.

For centuries, the practice of Kashmiri Shaivism seems to have been imparted by oral tradition as a doctrine to the aspirant seeking to test their self. The credit of putting the main principles in writing goes to Vasugupta, who is said to have lived towards the end of the eighth or the beginning of the ninth century AD.

Kashmiri Shaivism prescribes the four methods to obtain transcendence of the self—anavopaya, one that focusses on bodily consciousness, saktopaya, the method of focussing on awareness, sambhavopaya, the method of thoughtlessness, and anupaya, the 'methodless' method for spiritual practices to attain moksha or salvation.

Anyone, irrespective of caste, sex, religion, marital status or culture is allowed to undertake these spiritual practices as a way of leading a peaceful, spiritual and prosperous life.

Sufism as a form of mysticism is also at the heart of Kashmir's composite culture. At the core of Sufism lies the relationship between God and man, which is bound by love. From the relationship between God and man springs the ideas of ishq (divine love), fanaa (self-annihilation) and baqaa (abiding God). Thus, Sufis believe in one God who can be approached by man with utmost devotion, the spirit of renunciation and a loving heart.

LAL DED AND KASHMIRIYAT

I believe that the core value of our Kashmiriyat (synergic culture) was inspired by the verses of Lal Ded. She was a devout follower of Kashmiri Shaivism. The verses of Lal Ded became the inspiration for Sufis and saints who came to Kashmir. For over three hundred years, Lal Vaakhs were orally transmitted from one generation to another. The leading Sufi figure, Sheikh Nuruddin, also known as Nand Rishi, was highly influenced by Lal Ded. Lal Ded, along with Rishi Nuruddin, sowed the seeds for the Rishi order of saints, thus giving rise to many Rishi-saints. One Kashmiri folk story recounts that as an infant Rishi Nuruddin refused to be breastfed by his mother and was instead breastfed by Lal Ded.

Lal Ded was a strong critic of idolatry and saw it as a useless and even silly 'work' which adjured the worshipper of stocks and stones to turn to yogic doctrines and exercise for salvation.

> Idol is of stone; temple is of stone;
> Above (temple) and below (idol) are one;
> Which of them wilt thou worship, O foolish Pandit?
> Cause thou the union of mind and soul.[5]

She further castigated the fanatical followers of the so-called 'religions' by saying:

> O mind, why hast thou become intoxicated at another's expense?
> Why hast thou mistaken true for untrue?
> Thy little understanding hath made thee attached to other's religion;
> Subdued to coming and going; to birth and death.[6]

Lal Ded's spiritual vision was universal. Through her verses she advised against equating religious rituals with spirituality. Her mantra of universal harmony, brotherhood and universal divinity spoken during her lifetime can be applied to address the existential problems in South Asia and all over the globe. Above all, there was congruence between Shaivism and Sufism, as both believed in communication between man and God. This laid the foundation for what is referred to as Kashmiriyat, but some also call it lihaaz.[7] Though not the majority, some people have begun describing Kashmiriyat as some sort of lihaaz, which means being tolerant and respectful of diverse narratives and people of different faiths.

GROWING UP AMIDST FAITH

My mother, Sheila Dhar, was the only child of her parents and was mostly self-taught. She had picked up the essence of Lal Ded's teachings at a young age. She remembered most of the Lal Vaakhs. The word 'vaakh' comes from the Sanskrit word 'vaak' and vaakhs are understood to be one of the oldest forms of verse in the Kashmiri language. My mother, during her lifetime, passed on some of these teachings to me. I would be amazed when my mother would recall Lal Vaakhs with such deep understanding that it did not need any formal education to appreciate its essence. Most difficult problems have simple answers if we believe in truth and universal divinity.

We are a Kashmiri Pandit family; all members of our lineage are originally inhabitants of the Valley. Since all Kashmiri Pandits were Brahmins, while growing up, I did not see the prevalence of the caste system in Kashmir as it exists in the rest of India. My father's house was in the Dhar Enclave at Nai Sarak, not far from where I was born. A Muslim midwife officiated at my birth. Despite being a Kashmiri Brahmin child, I was nursed by a Muslim lady, Khatija, who breastfed me for most of my childhood at the house of my maternal grandparents, close to the famous Ganesha temple, Ganpatyar. I called her dodh maej, or the mother who suckles. She became a sort of foster mother to me. I fondly remember her and retained my ties with her by visiting her house as I grew up. Our relationship, however, faded after we shifted to a new colony, and subsequently, as I moved out of Kashmir for schooling.

Kashmiri Pandits are Brahmins, but they never practise untouchability against the followers of other religions or castes. I used to see Kashmiri Brahmins drink water brought by Muslims and eat food cooked in a Muslim boat. In fact, it was usually a Muslim midwife who officiated at the birth of a Hindu child, and at death it was invariably a Muslim who arranged the pyre and supervised the cremation of a Hindu.

It is tradition for Kashmiri women to deliver babies at their parents' place; Sarla and Maharaj, my elder sister and brother, and younger siblings, Ravi and Vinod, too, were born in the same house. But I felt I had unquestioned rights over my dodh maej; none of my brothers and sisters were entitled to her love the way I was. I would protest if anyone tried to come close to her. A Hindu child growing up on the milk of a Muslim woman was just a usual part of our composite culture in the Valley during my childhood days. The Kashmiri Shaivite Hinduism and Sufi Islam as practised during our times helped create a deep belief in a composite culture, since Lal Ded preached:

Shiv chhuy thalyi thalyi rav zaan
Mav zaan hyond ti musalmaan
Trukh hay chhukh ti paani prazaan
Sway chhay tas siity zeenyiy zaan

[Shiva is always with you like the sun,
Do not discriminate between a Hindu and a Musalmaan;
If you are wise, try to know your self,
That alone is your knowledge of the Almighty.]

(How stupid…to discriminate between individuals—
Hindus and Muslims! If you are truly sensible, recognize
your own self. It will help you achieve the eternal truth.)[8]

As children, we would stand on the riverfront of Ganpatyar
School on the Jhelum to wave national flags to visiting dignitaries.
Colourful boat processions would be held on the Jhelum to
welcome VVIPs—it was like a festival. I recall, sometime around
July/August 1961, Jawaharlal Nehru visited Srinagar. Huge crowds
assembled on the river banks to greet him. The best of Kashmiri
carpets, shawls and even colourful bed sheets were displayed
from houses along the bank of the river, along with buntings
and banners. It is difficult to obliterate memories of this peaceful
paradise—vibrant images of colourful boats sailing under the
bridges of Srinagar, and people standing side by side, irrespective
of colour, creed, sex and religion, shouting slogans and hailing the
visiting dignitary. These images are still fresh in my mind. I was a
child waving a flag, shouting 'Chacha Nehru zindabad'. All of that
remains firmly etched in my psyche.

VIP or VVIP boat processions were rare, but it was common
to see boatmen sailing their cargo boats on the Jhelum and
singing together. Several Englishmen had mentioned to J.L. Kaul
(author of Kashmiri Lyrics, 1945) that they could catch the lilt
of Kashmiri songs more easily than in any song from any other
part of India. One such native of England, Mary Hallowes, who
visited Kashmir, caught the tune of 'Yaa illaa, laa illaa', a song of
boatmen rowing on the Jhelum:

Yaa illaa, laa illaa,
Kraaliaar, Baliaar!
Ya Peer, Dastgeer
Khaliko, Malik-ko!

[In the name of Allah or the Almighty,
And remembering our Peer Dastgeer,
Let us pull together with full strength to reach our
destination,
Be it Kraaliyaar or Baliyaar.]

She then created a boat song in English with a similar
tune:

Swift the current, dark the night,
Stars above our guide and light
All together on the rope
In our sinews lies our hope.[9]

We children were happy singing '*Ya Pir Dastgeer, Ya Pir Dastgeer*'.
As I grew up, I realized a Kashmiri Pandit or a Muslim swears by
Dastgeer if he is telling the truth. No one ever lies in the name of
Dastgeer. There is a 200-year-old Sufi shrine in Khanyar, Srinagar,
known as Dastgeer Sahib. Pandits and Muslims hold this shrine
in the highest respect.

Five decades later when I look back, I realize why I am at ease
while hearing diverse discourses on religions and visiting various
places of worship. I have been fortunate to visit Vatican City, the
Golden Temple, Somnath, Dwarka and mosques, and done ziyarats
in India and abroad. I have even been on the road crossing in
Makkah up to where non-Muslims are allowed. I have been driven
essentially by the belief in universal brotherhood. Perhaps for

me it could also be our deep roots in Kashmiri Shaivism. Swami Lakshmanjoo, one of the most well-known scholars of Kashmiri Shaivism in recent times, has often said in his discourses at Ishber Ashram in Srinagar that people should be self-aware, and that if one accepts that there is a 'God-consciousness' in everyone, it will be impossible to be hateful towards others—all would then be one. The state of self-awareness, or chaitanya, is an independent and eternal state beyond time and space.

In my present home in Kolkata, I often wonder where destiny has brought me to live my last years. This city, though the City of Joy for many, cannot replace home.

2

ORIGINS AND EARLY INHABITANTS

The accession of Kashmir to India in October 1947 is the predominant focus of most discourses on Kashmir. In the dust and heat of popular debates, people seldom look back at history and ask questions about the beginnings of Kashmir. As a young boy, I would be excited to hear folktales on Kashmir from my mother that had survived through oral tradition for thousands and thousands of years. One such folktale, 'Heemal and Nagrai', was of a period when Kashmir was a lake surrounded by mountains and full of water, and was called Satisar. It is a mystical tale of deep love of a serpent king, Nagrai, who had the power to assume human form, and a princess, Heemal.

Geologists attest that around 8000 BC, the Valley of Kashmir was a vast lake surrounded by mountains. The *Nilamata Purana*[10] of Sage Nila is the earliest source of information on the origin of Kashmir, its earliest inhabitants and its tirthas, or places of pilgrimage. It tells us how Lord Shiva drained off all the water from the lake by striking the mountain with his trishul (trident). The *Puranas* are the richest collection of mythology in the world.

Most of them attained their formal form around AD 500 but were passed on as oral tradition since the time of Krishna (about 3100 BC as per legend). The *Puranas* are an integral part of Indian cultural ethos; they serve as guidebooks for life and society in India. Subhash Kak, an eminent scholar, describes Kashmir as the centre of Puranic geography. As per Puranic conception, the earth's continents are arranged in the form of a lotus.

In *Kashmir and its People: Studies in the Evolution of Kashmiri Society*,[11] Kak writes that Mount Meru as per Puranic geography stands at the centre of the world—the pericarp or seed vessel of the flower, as it were—surrounded by a circular range of mountains. Around Mount Meru, like the petals of the lotus, are arranged four island continents (dvipas), aligned to the four points of the compass—Uttarakuru to the north, Ketumala to the west, Bhadrashva to the east and Bharata or Jambudvipa to the south. The meeting point of the continents is the Meru mountain, which is in the Himalayas.

In the Puranas, Kashmir is also referred to as a gerek (hill), nestled as it is in the hills. Kashmir had then been defined as 'a land, ruling in which is difficult'! This definition remains so relevant even today!

According to folklore, the drainer of this lake was an ascetic named Kashyapa, hence the reclaimed land was called Kashyap-pur or Kashyap-mar, and later, Kashmir. The name Kashmir also implies 'land desiccated from water', from the Sanskrit 'ka', meaning water, and ‹shimeera›, meaning desiccate. Others simply believe that the land came to be called Kashyapa Mir, or the lake of Sage Kashyap, while it was initially called Satisar.

I recall that on one of the school picnics we were taken to Burzahom, a prominent archaeological site, 16 km from school, in the north-east of Srinagar. In those days, it was customary for schools to take young children to Burzahom to enlighten them on the historical importance of our Valley.

In Kashmiri, Burzahom means 'birch', a species of tree. Excavations at Burzahom have confirmed the existence of a vibrant civilization in the Neolithic and Megalithic eras, a civilization that had well-established contacts with Central Asia and peninsular India. Some years back, I met a scientist at the Tata Institute of Fundamental Research (TIFR) in Mumbai who confirmed to me that TIFR had done radiocarbon tests on different samples of skulls unearthed at Burzahom. The tests confirmed that Kashmir was a civilization before the last quarter of the third millennium BC. The radiocarbon dates obtained from samples of Burzahom Neolithic sites range from 4325 ($\pm$120) BC to 3492 ($\pm$108) BC.[12]

If the *Nilamata Purana* is to be visualized in the contemporary context, there were four important Naga chiefs who ruled in the south, the west and the northern parts of Kashmir, with one amongst four being the Naga chief for the whole of Kashmir. In total, there are reportedly 527 Nagas who were worshipped, and four among them were important. The four dikpals, or deities, guarding the four Nagas were Bindusara in the east, Srimadaka in the south, Elapatra in the west and Uttaramanasa in the north. Later, the kingdom got divided into these four chief-ships and, interestingly enough, these Naga clans and their descendents wielded some power even up to the fourteenth century. The Nagas were the first inhabitants of the Valley and were worshippers of the sun and serpents.

Engagement with history has been part of the national heritage of the Kashmiris. As the former prime minister of India Jawaharlal Nehru put it, India learnt historiography from Kashmir. One of the first and authentic books of history in India was authored by Kalhana, the worthy son of Kashmir. Kalhana's *Rajatarangini* describes the occurrences in the Valley from ancient times to AD 1149–1150. It is written in verse and based on traditions, legends and inscriptions. The same historical sense prompted Sultan Zain-ul-Abideen to make his court historians record the events from early times up to his reign. Since then, several historical narratives of a high intellectual standard dealing with events up to the present day have been written in Kashmir. P.N.K. Bamzai in his book *A History of Kashmir* has introduced Kashmir and its cultural heritage to the world. It is a singular handbook of ancient, medieval and modern Kashmir.

'The great geographical boundary which separated Kashmir from the rest of India, coupled with the marked differences of climatic conditions, have, from early times, assured to the alpine land a distinct character of its own, which manifests itself strongly in all matters of culture, custom and social organization,' writes M.A. Stein, who translated Kalhana's *Rajatarangini* to English in AD 1900. It is this distinct character that was left untouched by hundreds of years of our trials and tribulations.

SEAT OF LEARNING

Apart from its scenic beauty, Kashmir has been looked upon with awe and appreciation for the high level of intellectual attainment of its men and women. Even today, in most parts of south India, Brahmins, in particular those of the Saraswat clan, acknowledge Kashmir as a seat of learning by chanting the hymn 'Namaste Sharda Devi Kashmir–Puravasini' (I bow before the Goddess Sharda who hails from Kashmir) as part of their morning prayers.

Around the sixth century BC, the Valley of Kashmir seems to have come under the influence of Bactrians, Scythians and the Parthians, as it was part of the Gandhara region in north-west Pakistan. Cyrus the Great had risen to power to rule Persia, Afghanistan and regions of northern India. Around 326 BC, when Alexander marched with his army to India, small Greek chief-ships arose in the north-western region of India and Demetrious became the ruler of a big kingdom, which included Kashmir. Many coins of Greek rule have been found in the Valley. It is reported that Menander, a Greek chieftain, was defeated by a Naga sena in a religious discussion and became a Buddhist. Around 177 BC, the Kushanas occupied Gandhara and ruled Kashmir around the first century AD. They found many stupas, towns and viharas (monasteries) in the Valley.

It was during the powerful reign of the Kushana king Kanishka that the Fourth Buddhist Council was held in Kashmir. Kashmir adopted Buddhism and became the fountainhead for spreading Buddhism in Central Asia, China, Tibet and Southeast Asia. The Mahayana or northern Buddhism (Great Vehicle) born in Kashmir benefited from the knowledge, wisdom and philosophy of Kashmiri Shaivism as practised by Kashmiri scholars. People were not happy with the archaic and complicated rites and rituals of Brahmins and powerful upper castes. Ashoka visited Kashmir twice and left 5,000 monks for the study and propagation of his doctrine.

Vairocana was the first Kashmiri missionary who built a Buddhist vihara at Khotan in Central Asia. Kumarajiva, Buddhayasas, Sanghabuti and Vimalaksha spread Buddhism in Tibet and China. Gunavarman is renowned for introducing Buddhism in Java, Sumatra, Bali, Brunei and other islands in Southeast Asia. Kashmiri scholars wrote Buddhist texts and literature in Sanskrit in contrast with the rest of India which wrote in Pali. Sanskrit was written in the Kharosthi and the Brahmi script. However, Kashmiri scholars developed a script of their own—the Sharada—which, though differing from Devanagari in certain details, follows it in essence. The Tibetans who had no script for their language adopted the Sharada script of Kashmir around the ninth century AD. This historical legacy of Kashmir in spreading spiritualism and harmony was the bedrock of Kashmiri ethos.

It was around the seventh century AD that Buddhism started losing its popularity to Hinduism. Patronage extended by some kings to Hinduism helped it assert its dominant position. Hinduism became popular also because Kashmir had evolved its own brand of humanistic philosophy known as Kashmiri Shaivism. Scholars had evolved a monistic philosophy which was quite distinct from the *Advaita Vedanta* followed by Hindus elsewhere. They taught that phenomenal existence, though transient in nature, was not unreal, and one could try to integrate oneself through sadhana into one non-dual parama Shiva.

Abhinavagupta propounded a new philosophy of Kashmiri Shaivism which became popular as Trika philosophy. This newly propounded philosophy represented a synthesis of all previous spiritual discourses and canons, and dealt with all human beings irrespective of caste and creed; it had all the features to qualify as 'scientific humanism'. It drew many Buddhists into its fold. Consequently, a burgeoning number of Buddhist shrines became centres of the new learning.

The successive Karkota and Utpala dynasties each produced great kings, like Lalitaditya (AD 724–761) and Avantivarman (AD 855–883), respectively, whose fabled military exploits and colossal contribution to making Kashmir a flourishing literary centre and a politically stable and economically prosperous region have immortalized them in the annals of history. The Lohara dynasty that succeeded the Utpala dynasty also produced a remarkable woman leader, Queen Didda (AD 981–1003). Despite being censured in history as unscrupulous, Didda ruled the Valley with a resolve that contributed to its stability and prosperity. The glorious years of Hindu rule reached its peak during the reign of the illustrious King Harsha (AD 1089–1101).[13] At the outset, it must be clarified that King Harsha of Kashmir should not be confused with King Harshavardhana of Kannauj, also popularly known as King Harsha, who ruled northern India from 606–647 CE. Kalhana's *Rajatarangini* gives an interesting account of King Harsha. However, the sinister side of his character overpowered his benevolent side, which resulted in expensive and futile military expeditions, plunders and ecological disasters compounded by flood and famine. The consequence, not hard to surmise, was the unceremonious end of Harsha's life at the hands of his rebellious subjects.

Muslim contact with Kashmir had commenced as early as the eighth century AD, when Mohammad Bin Qasim planned to invade Kashmir in AD 713 but failed in his mission. This was followed by another Arab invasion in AD 757-758 which, too, met a similar fate. By that time, Kashmir had emerged as a place of refuge for some Muslims. Between AD 1015 and AD 1021, Mahmud of Ghazni, too, failed to seize Kashmir. His army plundered the southern part of the Valley and forcibly converted some inhabitants to Islam.

Muslim expatriate soldiers of fortune and merchants formed the core of early Muslim settlers in Kashmir. One such adventurer was Shah Mir, who arrived from Swat Valley in Central Asia to Kashmir in AD 1313. The armies of the Islamized Mongol, under Zulju, a Mongol chieftain, invaded Kashmir in AD 1320 and reduced it to a battered state before leaving.

Rinchan, a Buddhist prince from Ladakh, had revolted

against his uncle, the ruler of Ladakh, and had fled the region, defeated. Suhadeva, a weak king, was then the ruler of Kashmir. He gave refuge to Rinchan, appointing him as his minister. Then Suhadeva had to flee to Tibet, defeated by the Mongols under Dulchu, a Tatar chief. His able prime minister and commander-in-chief, Ramachandra, took over and appointed Rinchan as his prime minister. Then Rinchan became ambitious. He took advantage of the situation in Kashmir. He sent several hundred armed men defeat Ramachandra and killed him, taking his family as prisoners. Kota Rani was the daughter of Ramachandra. Rinchan married Kota Rani, but was not allowed to convert to Hinduism as he had murdered Ramachandra. He converted to Islam, assuming the name of Sadruddin Shah, to gain the support of the people and legitimize his rule (AD 1320–1323).[14]

Rinchan's conversion to Islam heralded the dawn of Muslim rule in Kashmir, although it is customary to associate the beginning of the rule with the ascendancy of Shah Mir (AD 1339–1342), a foreigner from Swat Valley, to the throne of Kashmir. Shah Mir had come to the Valley in pursuit of a dream in which he had been told by a holy man that he would succeed to the throne of Kashmir. He had come to the Valley with his family and relatives from Swat, Central Asia. Shah Mir proclaimed himself Sultan Shamsuddin in 1339. With this proclamation Shah Mir's dynasty was established, which was to last for 222 years until it was toppled by the mighty Mughals. While the dynasty flourished for quite some time, rot began to set in from the time of Sultan Sikandar, whose rule coincided with Taimur's invasion. As the impending threats of his invasion loomed larger, the meek Sikandar receded into the background and let his officials display their religious bigotry against the Hindus for the first time in the history of Kashmir. Hindu temples were seized, idols broken and jizya tax imposed on the Hindus. It was during this phase that the first exodus of Kashmiri Pandits from the Valley took place.

AT ITS GLORIOUS BEST

It was only after Zain-ul-Abidin of the Shah Mir dynasty took over as the sultan of Kashmir in AD 1420 that some semblance of communal harmony was restored. Zain-ul-Abidin's reign was a remarkable phase of peace, prosperity and religious cooperation. It was the phase when Kashmiriyat was at its glorious best. Abidin was fondly referred to as 'Bud Shah' or the 'Great King'. For about two centuries after the accession of the first Muslim king to rule Kashmir, the administration was carried out by the local traditional Brahmin class, the Kashmiri Pandits, with Sanskrit as the court language. However, Abidin's successors could not match up to his glory, as has often happened in history. Thus, there was another protracted period of political instability that harboured corruption and intrigue, providing ample opportunities for mightier political forces to jump into the fray and call the shots.

At the time when Babur made his appearance on the political horizon of Delhi, Kashmir was rattled by conflicts between the Magre and Chak clans. During Humayun's time, Mirza Haider, a Turk, occupied Srinagar in 1540 AD with the help of Mughal forces sent by the emperor, but refrained from crowning himself the king. Placing a weakling, Nazuk Shah, on the throne, Haider remained the *de facto* ruler of Kashmir for eleven years. By the time Akbar came to power, Kashmir had become a much-coveted territory for the emperor, who looked for an opportune moment to seize it. The opportunity came when Yousuf Shah Chak, a young and irresolute sultan, rose to power following his father's untimely death and was immediately exposed to nefarious schemes devised by his rivals to oust him. One of them was Lohar Chak, who succeeded in replacing him for a brief spell, and as fate would have it, pushed Yousuf Shah towards seeking help from Akbar. But Yousuf Shah tried double-crossing Akbar by entering into a secret deal with Lohar Chak. Akbar did not take this lightly. On the fateful day of 28 March 1586, the Kashmiri sultan was forced to accept Mughal sovereignty, thus marking the end of Kashmir's independence. Kashmir was drawn to the vortex of imperial rule in Delhi.

While Akbar was tolerant towards the Hindus—with the Kashmiris looking at him with great fondness and hope as though he were another Zain-ul-Abidin—Aurangzeb's bigotry once again dealt a crushing blow to the solidarity that Akbar and his successors, Jahangir and Shah Jahan, had delicately managed to build and consolidate. The end of Mughal rule offered little respite to the Kashmiris, for it was to be replaced by the much-dreaded sixty-seven years of Afghan rule. It was an agonizing period of relentless despotism, inter-religious wars, inter-clan conflicts and major famines that transformed the paradise on earth into a living hell. The brutal oppression perpetrated by the Afghans caused irreparable damage to the Hindus and Shias, and left indelible scars on the Kashmiri psyche as a whole. Little did we know that the Sikhs who would replace the Afghans would do little to assuage our pain.

Any tourist who visits Kashmir is mesmerized by the beauty of the Mughal Gardens. The Mughals built many things in Kashmir for posterity. Akbar built the Hari Prabhat fort; Jahangir built the gardens in Shalimar, Nishat and Verinag; Noor Jehan built Achabal; Shah Jahan built Chashma Shahi; and Dara Sikoh built Pari Mahal.[15]

Kashmir came under Sikh rule in 1819, with the charismatic Ranjit Singh at the helm of affairs. Pandit Birbal Dhar, a revenue collector under the last Afghan governor Mohammad Azam Khan, took the initiative of seeking the help of Sikh rulers to save Kashmiris from the unspeakable cruelties of the Afghans. The beginning of Sikh rule in Kashmir marked the end of Muslim rule in the region. While that meant the end of oppression of the Hindus at the hands of Muslim rulers, Sikh rule introduced discriminatory policies directed at the Muslims. Thus, what the Kashmiri Muslims now faced at the hands of Sikh rulers was what the Kashmiri Hindus had faced at the hands of Muslim rulers; either way, such sectarian policies did much to weaken the composite culture of the Kashmiris. When the Dogras succeeded the Sikhs, they were more interested in pleasing the British than making any spectacular turnaround for the prosperity of Kashmir.

While Gulab Singh managed to acquire the independence of Kashmir from the British in lieu of his unflinching loyalty to the crown and a payment of ₹75 lakhs, by the time India inched closer to independence, Kashmiris yearned for freedom from the shackles of the Dogra rule.

The British created the state of Jammu and Kashmir (J&K) through the sale of Kashmir to the Dogra raja of Jammu, Gulab Singh, by the Treaty of Amritsar, 1846. They wanted to create a ring of buffer states around their Indian dominion. They also helped Gulab Singh crush the revolt of the Kashmiris. The creation of J&K should be seen in the context of the prevailing Anglo-Russian rivalry in Central Asia and the increasing Russian interest and influence in the northwest frontiers of India. The British encouraged the Dogras to spy on the Russians, for which the first Russian school was established in Srinagar and spies were sent out into Russian territories. As Kashmir acquired importance in the context of the Anglo-Russian strategy in Asia, the British constructed roads from Kohala in Abbottabad to Srinagar and Srinagar to Gilgit for military purposes. A British agency was also established in Gilgit.

The Treaty of Amritsar by which the British sold Kashmir to Gulab Singh for ₹75 lakhs was a sale deed. One can describe it as one of the most shameful sale transactions negotiated, which did not take into account the views of the Kashmiris. But this would be seeking retrospective morality, and it would be anachronistic to expect present 'civilized' behaviour to have prevailed then. Who ascertained the views of anyone unimportant, i.e. the people, in those days? This treaty made the Dogra raja of Jammu the maharaja of Jammu, Kashmir, Ladakh and Tibet, as a reward for service rendered by him to the British government. Perhaps it should be in order to demand an unqualified apology and expression of remorse from the British for this shameful act of their rule, where people were sold as if they were their bonded slaves. That may help heal a deep wound.

One striking fact that emerges is that the history of Kashmir is full of people who rose to great heights with respect to art, culture, religion and economic prosperity when they received impetus from outside rather than from inside the Valley—from mainland India, Indo-Greeks and Indo-Scythians. Ashoka's sovereign power extended to Kashmir. He had established friendly relations with Greece and Egypt. Our stone architecture and sculptures in the Valley are testimony to that. Kanishka, based in Kashmir, ruled from Central Asia to Bengal. During Lalitaditya's time (AD 724–760), Kashmir was in close contact with the rest of India. In fact, Lalitaditya had raised Kashmir to the heights of glory that it had never reached before. From here conquerors were to go forth to neighbouring kingdoms of Punjab and western India and bring them under the sway of Kashmir.

After Akbar established the rule of Mughals in Kashmir, access to market opportunities in India and Central Asia provided a fillip to economic growth.

The Damaras were the most important class in the ancient history of Kashmir. They were a class of feudal lords who controlled villages and could raise contingents of soldiers when the need arose. They established their stronghold in various parts of Kashmir with several kings at their mercy. Thus, their political power is not hard to guess. Like the barons of medieval England, they often defied the king's orders, and in times of unrest, royal authority could only be asserted using force.

Today's political families of Kashmir appear to be the new Damaras, powerful feudal landlords of the ancient and medieval era. Kashmir has always been at the mercy of chieftains who emerged from time to time to exploit the toiling masses. The tragedy of Kashmir and Kashmiris lies in the fact that history has repeated itself only too often, while the masses have remained ignorant of the machinations of the Damaras. The genetic pool from which the Pandits, Muslims, Buddhists and Sikhs of Kashmir hail is common, and so are their traits.

It is well established that the history of Kashmir is over 5,000 years old. Hence, looking at what has happened over the past fifty or sixty years may be equivalent to missing the wood for the trees. Kashmir was the centre of military, political and spiritual excellence and, historically, a linking hub for Central Asia, Tibet and the northern plains of India.

The poet Amir Khusrau who wrote about Kashmir did not comprehend or imagine that the paradise would be the envy of many countries later. It is for us to regain our paradise. And to help do that, we need to look within our own hearts and minds to find reasons why we are caught in such a vicious cycle as a society, century after century. Perhaps introspection will help us realize what 'being Kashmiri' means.

3

BEING KASHMIRI

We Kashmiris may seem complex to the world, and how! Of the many authors I have read, two were quite reasonable in understanding Kashmiris. It would be a shock to many, but Walter Roper Lawrence, the famous author of The Valley of Kashmir,16 who was the settlement commissioner in Kashmir from 1889–1895, said that Kashmiris did not strictly adhere to the truth, and attributed their misery to lying, and envy, or malice. A hundred years after Lawrence, A.S. Dulat, in his book *Kashmir—The Vajpayee Years*, wrote that Kashmiris were the most complex characters, who were not easy to fathom or engage with.

TO TRUST OR NOT TO TRUST?

One would imagine I, as a Kashmiri, would defend Kashmiris against this accusation, but listen to this first. Once, when I was a kid, my friend's uncle had admitted her brother to a school. The boy's date of birth was recorded as March 1955. A year later, the very same uncle accompanied my friend for admission and recorded her date of birth as July 1955. The teachers protested at the absurdity of the act but the uncle remained unperturbed in the face of such protests and was adamant about keeping my friend's date of birth as July 1955. The principal was compelled to ask the uncle to send her father to meet him, at which the uncle was enraged and retorted that the prevailing custom in Kashmir did not encourage differentiating between the uncle and the father. The principal naturally got angry and said, 'I only want to ask her father how he produced a child in only three months.' This calmed down the uncle who, however, kept insisting on recording her birth year as 1955, and his decision prevailed in the end.

Part II of the famous book *An Area of Darkness: His Discovery of India* by V.S. Naipaul[18] has three chapters devoted to his experience of travelling in Kashmir. The chapters titled 'A Doll's House in the Dal Lake', 'The Medieval City' and 'Pilgrimage' cover his stay in a houseboat named Hotel Liward on the Dal, his travels in Srinagar and his visit to Amarnath respectively. His interaction with Aziz and Mr Butt, two local characters, are vivid and reflective of our simplicity, flexibility as well as dishonesty to achieve our goals by the gift of the gab!

It is sometimes necessary to do some introspection and weigh the comments of two totally unrelated individuals, Naipaul and Lawrence, a century apart, who interacted with us as independent individuals with no malice or envy. Perhaps Lawrence is right when he says, 'Kashmir, as possessing a distinct nationality, character, language, dress and body customs, affords much that is interesting, while its unique history and curious administration are worth careful study.' Those who disregard this urge of Kashmir of seeking its own identity in a modern nation state are unlikely to address the real issues at hand in Kashmir.

While militancy brought loss of life and property, and changed the narrative of the future discourse in Kashmir, it also highlighted the core elements of simplicity of local Kashmiris that were brought into focus by security personnel who believed in the rule of law. Discussion with some senior officers from the defence forces who served in Kashmir in the early 90s at the peak of militancy reveals a less understood trait from the two anecdotes shared with me.

Till about early or mid-1996, before the situation was fully stabilized, all civil jails and sub-jails were full of militants, which forced the government to allow some army units to set up sub-jails in their own headquarters. Normally, as per the law, any individual picked up for questioning or for being a suspected militant has to be handed over to the police and brought before the magistrate at the earliest, and not later than twenty-four hours. A sub-jail meant that any militant picked up would be taken to the police for the lodging of an FIR. After being brought before the magistrate, he would be remanded to judicial custody, which meant he would be brought back and lodged in the sub-jail. Sub-jails held about twenty-five to thirty prisoners, all of whom were militants and lodged in two large tents surrounded by barbed wire. These jails were run exactly as all other jails and all procedures that could be followed without compromising their security were followed.

There was a separate tent where they could meet their families once a week, and since they were under trial with physical evidence already established against them (in terms of weapons in their possession, etc.), there was no scope of interrogating them. Also, they did not provide any intelligence inputs once they had been caught, as militants shifted location. The army, however, felt that there was a possibility that some of them could have information which, while not having action value, would help as background. To get this information, the army put microphones in their tents, including the visitors' tent. All these microphones were voice-activated. As a result, they found that when a prisoner met his family, he generally gave the latest inputs about other active militants from his group. While that really was never up-to-date information, it helped the army construct very detailed organizational and individual sketches of the militants still active.

This background information came in use particularly when the army caught either suspected militants or overground workers. Their interrogators were able to use the information they had, to confirm other information. The army also sounded very knowledgeable, which created grave doubts in the minds of those they had picked up as to the exact information they had on them. In a number of cases, such specific knowledge had broken the spirit of the militant, and he had spilled whatever information he had.

For this procedure, one of the intelligence officers decided to make use of technology. In their interrogation room, he set up a desktop computer in one corner behind a screen with a dot matrix printer connected to it. On the other side of the screen, he kept a chair for the prisoner under interrogation. He got hold of some cables used in ECG machines, and set them up, so it looked as if they were attached to the computer behind the screen. He made the prisoner sit down and attach the suction cups on the cables to his forehead and chest. They had a white coatsoldier sitting on the computer. Then the interrogator commenced asking questions. Through experience, the officer already knew signs that suggested the prisoner was lying. So, while asking a question, if he felt the prisoner was lying, discreetly signalled to the computer operator, who then immediately started the printer, which, being dot matrix, started to chatter.

The interrogator immediately accused the prisoner of lying and started making threats. Soon enough, the prisoner came to believe that the 'truth machine' always caught a lie. It was then only a matter of a few hours of interrogation before he broke down and gave them all the information he had. This was a simple but effective method to gain information, including intelligence that the army were able to obtain and use to fight terrorism. In fact, the reputation of the machine spread in the villages, and anybody they caught mostly volunteered to give information straightaway to avoid being attached to the 'truth machine'.

Once an army officer threatened a militant, who was caught at his girlfriend's house, that he would put him through the Machine Test with his wife as witness. He was quite cooperative after that. He was located across the Banihal Pass and was used as a spotter. The army caught many militants who were trying to sneak out of the Valley in apple trucks so that they could avoid the Valley in winter.

In 1996, when elections were being conducted, the army was not involved in any way in protecting booths as election personnel. They only carried out intense patrolling in their areas of responsibility to ensure there were no militant attacks. On election day, they had a problem in Shopian, where nobody was voting, as some people had gathered in the main mosque and were using the public address(PA) system to tell people not to vote. So, a senior army officer went to the mosque and entered with three army men, including a Kashmiri, and met the maulvi. He told the maulvi that they did not care if they voted, but that they could not use the PA system to stop others. The maulvi refused the officer's request to stop, so the army just photographed everybody in the mosque. Within fifteen minutes, the PA system was switched off, the news spread and voting commenced. All those sitting inside the mosque insisted on meeting the senior army officer the next day to show him the ink on their fingers to prove they had indeed voted.

KASHMIRIS VERSUS NON-KASHMIRIS

Twenty years later, as experienced in the Lok Sabha elections in Srinagar in April 2017, social media added a new dimension to creating an environment of fear and threat. Looking at some of the video messages that were streamed on Facebook, WhatsApp and other formats of modern media communication, any person concerned with the safety of his family and property opted to stay indoors. No wonder the polling percentage of elections urned out to be the lowest ever, less than 7 per cent. What had changed in two decades was the supremacy of social media in establishing a new narrative.

We are Kashmiris if we have a typical nose and baldness. Perhaps our men become bald much earlier than their counterparts elsewhere in the world. We love food. Wazwan is a delight. No offence to other food lovers in the world, but we Kashmiris take our love for food a little too seriously.

We have some sort of pride. We wish the human race could be divided into two groups: people who are Kashmiris and people who wish they were Kashmiris. In recent decades, many inter-caste, interfaith and international marriages have taken place in the Kashmiri community. We make it a point to tell the other family in the alliance how lucky they are to have married off their child or ward to someone from our community, irrespective of whether the other party is better off than us or not.

We get terribly excited to see a Kashmiri on television. Nidhi Razdan, Shereen Bhan, Aditya Raj Kaul and others who are regularly on TV make us feel proud. Even if a Kashmiri is seen standing in a frame, we feel excited. *Koshur chu, Koshur chu* (he is a Kashmiri), we exclaim.

Whether you are a Muslim, a Sikh or a Pandit, every Kashmiri is related to the other, maybe as a cousin or a second cousin. I relish trying to find out connections and always end up finding one. We are born in the Valley known for Kashmiri apples but we seldom eat them. We make handicrafts and love watching artefacts in shops, but seldom buy them.

But it seems that we do not learn or want to learn from our past. History tells us that we can be the worst enemies of our own fate. It was we who invited the Afghans to oust Mughals, hoping that would lead us to peaceful times without atrocities. Later, it was we who invited the Sikhs to overthrow the Afghans, but our troubles continued.

Should we not retrospect in depth before inviting others to steer our destiny, and look within? Our well-wishers must also remember that Kashmir is still waiting for its rulers to give it a just and strong rule.

Lawrence writes in *The Valley of Kashmir*,[19] 'The Kashmiri is what his rulers have made him, but I believe and hope that two generations of a just and strong rule will transform him into a useful, intelligent and a fairly honest man.' We, Kashmiris, still await that moment in history.

4

UNCONTESTED PAST

The Lal Vaakh by Lal Ded quoted earlier in the first chapter invoked universal divinity by stressing that there is no difference between a Hindu and a Musalmaan. It was common to hear stories about our shared past and heritage, and how many Kashmiri Hindus retained their surnames after embracing Islam. It is normal to find common surnames between Kashmiri Pandits and Kashmiri Muslims. Kitchloo, Dar, Pandit, Wali, Raina, Mattoo, Reshi, Peer, Mirza, Durrani, Munshi, Parimoo and Bhat are some of the typical surnames in Kashmir.

We share the same ancestry. Sheikh Abdullah, the tallest leader of Kashmir post 1930s, came from a Kashmiri Pandit lineage. According to Mohi-ud-Din Sufi, author of the celebrated historical work, *Kashir: Being a History of Kashmir,* a Kashmiri Brahmin converted to Islam during the Afghan rule in 1766 and assumed the name of Sheikh Mohammad Abdullah.[20] His ancestors came from Rajwar. Another version is that Sheikh Abdullah's ancestors were Kashmiri Pandits of the Dattatreya Kaul family, who were high-caste Brahmins. His grandfather, Sheikh Ghulam Rasool, was the son of Ragho Ram Kaul.

MOHAMMAD IQBAL AND THE TWO-NATION THEORY

Mohammad Iqbal, the great poet who became famous as Allama Mohammad Iqbal, too, came from a Kashmiri Pandit clan that had converted to Islam much later. He came from the Sapru family of Sialkot. Kanhai Lal, Allama Iqbal's grandfather, was married to Poshi, who was named Indrani by her in-laws. They had three sons and five daughters. The three sons were Ratan Lal, Iqbal's father, Behari Lal and Nand Lal. Ratan Lal fell in love with a Muslim girl in the neighbourhood and married her. The family disowned him and Ratan Lal converted to Islam as Nur Mohammad.

As per family records of the Sapru family, Iqbal sought a reconciliation with the family. He met his grandmother, Indrani, and in a moving tone told her that the Sapru family blood ran through his veins. But since he was born to a Muslim mother, neither their family nor the Pandit biradari would accept them back. The Kashmiri Pandit samaj was bitterly divided. He, too, seemed to have been unhappy with his father, as he told his grandmother, Indrani.[21] She was all tears, but social taboos prevailed and she could not accept him back. For many days after Iqbal left, Indrani continued to feel as if he was sitting beside her. It is interesting to speculate what could have shaped the destiny of the subcontinent had the family accepted Iqbal back into the Pandit family.

Iqbal was always proud of his Hindu past but had nothing to say about his relations. The hurt of non-acceptance must have left a deep emotional impression on him. 'As often happens, the first generation of converts become more kattar than others. Iqbal thus grew up to be a devout Muslim,' wrote Khushwant Singh in his post, 'Iqbal's Hindu Relations' in *The Telegraph*. Thus, the kattar, devout Muslim became the principal ideologue of what later became Pakistan.[22]

There was not a single forum in Lahore where Kashmiri Muslims could utter their woes. However, in the early years of the last century, some sympathetic Kashmiri Muslim migrants established an association called the Kashmiri Conference. Sir Mohammad Iqbal was among its founding fathers. It was at this conference that Iqbal read this poignant poem on Kashmir:

> *Panja-e-zulm-o-jahalat ne bura haal kiya*
> *Bun ke miqraz hamein be-par-o-baal kiya*
> *Tor us dast-e-jafa-kesh ko Yarabb jis ne*
> *Ruh-e-aazadi-e-Kashmir ko pamaal kiya*

> [Oppression and ignorance hold us under their claws
> Our wings have been clipped as if by scissors
> God, break the hands of the persecutor
> Who rides roughshod on Kashmir's soul!][23]

Iqbal passed away on 21 April 1938, nine years before Pakistan became a reality. He became a barrister from Lincoln's Inn in London in 1906 and earned a doctorate in Philosophy from the University of Munich, Germany, in 1908. The poetry and philosophy of Rumi had a deep influence on his mind. Deeply grounded in religion since childhood, he studied culture and history of the Islamic civilization and its political future.

Iqbal was unhappy with the lack of unity amongst leaders of the Muslim League. He prevailed upon Mohammad Ali Jinnah to give up his self-imposed exile in London, return to India and lead the Muslim League. While Iqbal supported the idea of Muslim-majority provinces in 1930, Jinnah did not embrace the goal of

Pakistan until after the death of Iqbal.

In his letter dated 21 June 1937, Iqbal shared his vision of a separate Muslim state with Jinnah. 'A separate federation of Muslim provinces, reformed on the lines I have suggested above, is the only course by which we can secure a peaceful India and save Muslims from the domination of non-Muslims. Why should not the Muslims of north-west India and Bengal be considered nations entitled to self-determination just as other nations in and outside India are?'[24]

Iqbal had already in his presidential address to the Muslim League on 29 December 1930 outlined a vision of an independent state for Muslim-majority provinces in north-western India, but since J&K was independent, exclusion of Kashmir from his speeches was noteworthy. Iqbal became the first politician to propagate the two-nation theory.

The word 'Pakistan' did not figure in the presidential address of Iqbal either in Lahore in 1930 or in Allahabad in 1932. It was on 28 January 1933 that the idea of political separation was suggested by Choudhary Rahmat Ali, a Punjabi student in Cambridge. Choudhary and his three colleagues rejected the idea of a federation and demanded the creation of a separate homeland for Muslims. Pakistan was created as an acronym (PAKSTAN) by him to represent five northern units of India, **P**unjab, Northwest Frontier (**Af**ghan) Province, **K**ashmir, **S**ind and Baluchis**tan**. The pamphlet was titled 'Now or Never—Are we to live or perish for ever?'[25] The alphabet 'I' was added later for better pronunciation, as in Afghan-i-stan. This was how the term 'PAKISTAN' was coined and it later became both a Persian and an Urdu word meaning 'Land of the Pure'. This was an imaginary grouping of regions, with Islam as the binding force. Iqbal and Jinnah may have dissed the thought of the two-nation theory after this narrative came into the public domain.

However, Aslam Khan Khattak, one of the three students who wrote the pamphlet 'Now or Never', proposing Pakistan, went to London to call on Jinnah, who was practising law there in the early 1930s. Jinnah told him that he had read the pamphlet and was very unhappy about it. He said to Aslam Khan,[26] 'Why destroy the one great and good thing the British had done in India by unifying the heterogeneous elements into a united whole? Muslims and Hindus have to learn to live as friends and brothers.' Secondly, Choudhary had envisaged in his paper that 'This Muslim Federation of north-west India would provide the bulwark of a buffer state against invasion of India either with ideas or with arms from any quarter.'[27] Sadly, later events have proven both assumptions to be deeply flawed.

About a decade later, on 22 March 1940, Jinnah in his presidential address to the Lahore session of the Muslim League made it clear that the British and the 'Hindus' had failed to understand that common nationality was not possible for the Hindu and Muslim communities. Islam and Hinduism were not merely religions, but 'different and distinct social orders... They neither intermarry nor inter-dine and indeed they belong to two different civilizations which are based on conflicting ideas and conceptions.'[28]

COMMON LEGACY

Thankfully, this is what did not apply to Kashmir. We have a common language amongst Muslims and Hindus. I share the same culture, music and food habits with Muslims and have recollections of brotherhood and solidarity. Shivaratri is the most important festival in the annual calendar of Kashmiri Hindus.

It is called Herath and it is customary for children to receive tokens in the form of money as blessings from elders. Me and my siblings were pampered by colleagues of my father, mostly Muslims, who would make it a point to visit us and give their blessings. In particular, I can never forget late Uncle Lone, who used to secretly give me the highest amount in recognition of the fact that I was studying outside Kashmir. I last met Uncle Lone and his wife at the residence of their son in Jeddah, Saudi Arabia, in 1996, when I was working there on an assignment and they were performing Umrah pilgrimage. He blessed me when I reminded him of his visits to our house and treated me to a sumptuous meal. His sons, Dr Shafqat and Zafar, would often enquire after my father until he passed away last year. I am sure our parents must be blessing us from their heavenly abodes.

Sarwar Dar, Amrit Pal Singh and I were students of Civil, Mechanical and Chemical Engineering disciplines respectively at the Regional Engineering College, Srinagar (now NIT). We lived in close proximity in Rajbagh, Wazir Bagh and Jawahar Nagar, respectively, and continue to be as close as we were about five decades ago. My friends would visit our home during Shivaratri to enjoy Kashmiri delicacies. It was not unusual for Sarwar Dar to take home a parcel of cooked fish as a delicacy for his mother. Similarly, I would look forward to the annual feast, wazwan, during Eid at Sarwar's house to enjoy delicacies, especially gushtaba, a mutton dish of minced meat with yoghurt gravy. Skipping a meal each before and after the feast was my secret to enjoying a rich and heavy wazwan meal to the fullest.

Going back to the political scenario, Kashmiris led by Sheikh Mohammad Abdullah and the leaders of the National Conference wanted to maintain their secular ethos and did not see eye to eye with Jinnah's version of the two-nation theory.

Iqbal gave Sheikh Abdullah self-confidence, self-awareness and that affability with which he inspired his companions in their darkest moments and helped them negotiate rough patches in the path to freedom.

Forty years later, as the creation of Bangladesh has shown us, Islam has been unable to unite contiguous areas, such as in the Middle East and North Africa, as one nation. It, too, has failed the proposition that religion alone can be the basis for modern nation states. In my travels through nations in north Africa and the Middle East, I have seen various Muslim nation states with different interpretations and the practise of Islam and governance processes, from absolute monarchies to evolving democracies.

Sheikh Abdullah, in his autobiography *The Blazing Chinar*,[29] has touched upon establishing dominions on the basis of religions. Abdullah told Jinnah that establishing states on the basis of religions in India would fragment the country, and advised him against it. Reforms that benefitted everyone, irrespective of religion, was his preference.

Kashmir in the past three decades has been through the worst of times, with great loss of life and property. Our core values and beliefs are being tested by God. I pity those who do not want to learn from history and need to be reminded of Verse 39 of Book I of *Rajatarangini*, which says: 'That country may be conquered by spiritual merits, but not by forces of soldiers. Hence its inhabitants are afraid only of the world beyond.'[30]

I hope what has happened in the past thirty-five years is seen in history as just another aberration, and that the Valley returns to its glorious period of composite culture as it existed under the rule of Bud Shah and Akbar.

Kashmir has had an uncontested past. Kashmiri Hindus and Kashmiri Muslims share a common legacy. It is for us now to shape our destiny by leveraging this legacy of composite culture to prepare the ground for a happy, safe and prosperous pathway for our future generations.

5

MYSTERY OF THE HOLY RELIC

Bakshi Ghulam Mohammad was a politician of the National Conference and second in command to Sheikh Abdullah. He was the deputy prime minister of J&K from 1947–1953 and the prime minister from 1953–1964 when Sheikh Abdullah was imprisoned and dismissed by Jawaharlal Nehru for the Kashmir Conspiracy Case. He had relinquished the office of prime minister in October 1963 under the Kamaraj Plan. On 2 October 1963, the chief minister of Tamil Nadu, K. Kamaraj, had resigned to work for the Congress party. He had proposed to Jawaharlal Nehru, then prime minister of India, that all senior Congress leaders resign from their posts and devote time and energy for the revitalization of the Congress party. This proposal came to be known as the 'Kamaraj Plan'. Khwaja Shams-ud-din had taken over from Bakshi and remained the prime minister for a brief period of time from October 1963 to February 1964. It was during his time that the Prophet's relic was stolen from the Hazratbal shrine. Something terrible was happening and we were told to remain indoors.

My family had thought after the 1962 Indo-China War that

nothing as bad could ever happen to Kashmir again. It was imaginably the most disastrous event in their lives.

Trath and pralay were two words that my maternal grandmother would shout at any sign of threat to normalcy. 'Trath' means devastation and 'pralay' means big war. And then, mother and grandmother would do the most natural thing that has endured through generations—read 'Indrakshi Namsa Devi', a holy prayer, and chant loudly, invoking the blessings and the support of Devi to save Kashmir. Although my maternal grandmother still repeated trath and pralay, there was a prevailing anxiety that was considerably more palpable.

Moi-e-Muqqadas, the Prophet's relic, was stolen from the Hazratbal shrine on 27 December 1963. It caused a spontaneous stir. News of the theft spread like wildfire. *Chicago Tribune,* on 29 December, carried a headline, 'Moslems Riot over Theft of Sacred Relic', and it became international news. All across the Valley people came out to protest, but the focus area in the city was Lal Chowk.

Hazratbal is one of the holiest Muslim shrines in Kashmir. It is situated on the left bank of the Dal Lake in Srinagar. From 1972 to 1977, I had the good fortune of seeing the new mosque under construction while I was pursuing Chemical Engineering in the nearby National Institute of Technology (NIT). My friends Sarwar Dar and Amit Pal lived in a room shared by three people in the college hostel we called HMS Inn, signifying our composite heritage and secular ethos. I had put a poster on our door that said 'HMS Inn'. We often went from home to college together during semesters when we studied as day scholars. Like most Kashmiris of my generation, I have the same respect for the shrine as I have for Kheer Bhawani temple or the Sharika Devi temple on Hari Parbat. Every time I passed my semester examinations and received my merit scholarship, it was a practice to make a token offering from scholarship earnings at the shrine. Its green lawns were a place of relaxation for us while walking from the old campus to the new one. We could see the Nishat Bagh just across, and would hire a boat. We would ask to row the boat ourselves, promising to return it on time. But, often, the rowing of over two miles from Hazratbal to Nishat Bagh would drain us and we would leave the boat in Nishat Bagh itself. Boatmen at Hazratbal knew this and always had plans in place for such contingencies. One of them would bring all such boats back every time. Next time we would promise not to repeat such a thing, but they always understood. Our understanding was perfect. We would pay for one way only.

According to legend, the holy relic in Hazratbal was first brought to India by Syed Abdullah, a descendent of Prophet Mohammad. Syed Abdullah had settled in Hyderabad in 1635. Upon his death, his son inherited the relic and sold it to a wealthy Kashmiri businessman, Khwaja Nur-ud-Din Eshai. Inayat Begum, daughter of Khwaja Nur-ud-Din Eshai, established the shrine and became the custodian of the relic. After marriage into the Banday family of Kashmir, her descendents from the Banday family became the keepers of the relic, known as Nishaandehs.[31]

THE NIGHT OF 26 DECEMBER

Prior to this shocking incident, the relic had been displayed on 20 December for public reverence by the late Abdur Rahim Shah Banday. On 26 December, Banday sahib arranged for an influential person to have a private viewing of the relic. During this time of the year, Kashmir is awfully cold. According to reports, that night there was no one else present in the shrine.

The next day, early in the morning, when Rahim Sahib arrived at
the shrine, he got the shock of his life as he saw that the lock of
the room had been broken and the chest inside empty of the relic.
The news spread like wildfire across the state. Even though it was
snowing, thousands of men, women and children poured out into
the streets wailing and grieving. Life came to an abrupt halt and
the administration was paralysed.

Sheikh Abdullah was in prison for over ten years. India was
witnessing a new dawn in Kashmir politics. There was anger
against Bakshi Ghulam Mohammad. An entirely religious matter
was soon turning into a political movement, for or against Sheikh
Abdullah. Two politicians on the scene, Mir Qasim and G.M.
Sadiq, tried to douse the fire. They visited Hazratbal. Dr Karan
Singh appealed to Hindus and Sikhs to pray for the return of the
relic at temples and gurudwaras.

A 'Sacred Hair Action Committee' under Moulana Syed
Masoodi was set up by protesting Kashmiris. Farooq Abdullah
and Mirwaiz Maulvi Farooq jointly protested against the theft. It
marked the start of the journey for the 19-year-old Maulvi Farooq
in public life and the launch of the Sheikh's son in active public
movements. It was also my first exposure to Kashmiri protests.

Soon after having breakfast consisting of Kashmiri naan and
kahwa, I sneaked out of my house on some pretext to see what
exactly was happening in Lal Chowk. I recalled that discussions
at home with father and grandmother always brought up Lal
Chowk. Wearing a Kashmiri pheran and winter shoes, I also
carried a kangri to keep warm. A kangri is a versatile fire pot
of immense utility to Kashmiris in winters. Apart from keeping
warm, it is used for boiling eggs, drying socks and children's
clothes and burning isband (incense); elderly people also use it
as a spit pot.

There were not many people on the way from Jawahar Nagar to Lal Mandi, except a couple of tongas or horse-drawn carriages. I walked past Amira Kadal and did find some shops open, but business was almost nil. Somehow, I gathered enough courage to cross Amira Kadal to reach Lal Chowk. There used to be a cinema hall in Lal Chowk named Palladium. Many of us in Kashmir have seen movies of our favourite star, Dilip Kumar, in this theatre, especially during winter holidays.

A group of teenage boys and some elderly people soon came from Maisuma as well as from a side lane near Hotel Majestic. They started throwing stones at the police. Initially, the police ignored them, but as the intensity increased, I could see the police grouping together for what I later learnt was a lathi charge. I ran towards the gurudwara for shelter and saw one protester throwing his kangri at the charging policemen.

At the gurudwara, one Sikh gentleman asked me why I had ventured out. I left my kangri at the gurudwara, mustered up enough strength and ran the fastest race possible at that age, back via Amira Kadal and Lal Mandi, to my house in Jawahar Nagar.

We got to hear the next day that the Moi-e-Muqqadas, the holy relic, was brought back at night. Soon after its recovery, Radio Kashmir Srinagar interrupted its routine broadcast for Shams-ud-Din, the then premier, to share the message of prime minister Jawaharlal Nehru, and declared, 'Today is indeed Eid for us. I am happy to learn that the holy relic has been recovered. I send my hearty congratulations to you and to the people of Kashmir.' Muslims made for the mosques and Hindus blew conches; several thousands headed to Hazratbal for prayers.[32] Karan Singh declared prayers at all mosques, temples and gurudwaras. Usually the doors remain closed at night, but on that instance, for one night, it was left open. Policemen were stationed outside the mosque; the maulvis were permitted entry. This was done to ensure that no riot-like situation would arise.

When the holy relic was brought back, a lot of people said that it was not the original. Maulana Masoodi, using his powers of persuasion, got Syed Mirak Shah Kashani, a Sufi saint, and other respected persons, including Maulvi Mohammad Farooq, to identify it, and declared it to be genuine.

KASHMIR AT A STANDSTILL

Even after fifty years, no one knows who the real culprits were. It still remains a mystery. But when I met Colonel O.P. Bhatia (then retired) two years ago, I came to know something surprising. A young major of the Mountain Brigade in 1963–66, he told me his version of the tale. His unit was the 4th battalion of 3rd Gorkha Rifles known as 4/3GR. His brigade was posted near Avantipura and was called upon to maintain peace in the Valley during the crisis. He claims he was taught how to offer namaz as per associated rituals and wore civilian clothes. According to him, it was generally believed that Bakshi Ghulam Mohammad was apparently involved, as he and his mother had been in Jammu at that time. She fell sick and wanted to have a deedar (sight) of the relic. As she was sick and unable to travel to Hazratbal, Bakshi Ghulam Mohammad understandably promised to get the relic for her. However, as the stories spread that the relic had been taken to Jammu, there was unrest as people claimed that it was stolen.

Major Bhatia's unit was asked to conduct a peace march in the Valley. The perception was that it was being done for a good cause. So their work was to ensure peace.

He added that B.N. Mullick, the senior Intelligence Bureau

(IB) officer widely credited with the recovery of the relic, had assisted and facilitated the process of getting it back. Major Bhatia had one platoon of about thirty people with him. Other forces were placed a little outside but could be called when required. The team, led by Colonel Dilip Singh, his commanding officer, called on Dr Karan Singh in Raj Bhawan and congratulated them for maintaining peace in the Valley and for the recovery of the holy relic.

Many rumours abounded. One was from the Soviet Union accusing the CIA (Central Intelligence Agency) of the theft as an excuse to dismiss the state government; others suggested a conspiracy by Pakistan. It would help if we agree to what many believe was the genuine dying wish of an ailing old devout lady to have a deedar of the holy relic.

Bakshi Ghulam Mohammad, however, maintained that the theft was a diabolical political conspiracy against India and Kashmir to discredit the National Conference. Noted Indian journalist, Inder Malhotra, wrote in *The Indian Express* on 9 August 2010, about fifty years after reporting on the crisis, 'Apparently, a terminally ill lady in the Bakshi family wanted to have its deedar before dying. Unfortunately, its absence was noticed almost immediately.'[33]

However, the Hazratbal crisis had another important payoff. It made Nehru realize that Sheikh Abdullah could not be kept in jail any longer. He was released and recognized as an important political force to restore the confidence of Kashmiris to reach a political accord. Sheikh Abdullah visited Pakistan in May 1964, but the same month that he was there, Nehru passed away, on 27 May 1964. This sad news brought Kashmir to a standstill, and left it mourning, without its best well-wisher and tallest Kashmiri leader in the history of modern India.

6

TRUST ME, TRUST ME NOT

Right through the days described in *Rajatarangini*, mistrust between people at the helm governing Kashmir has been one of the major causes of tragedy that have befallen us from time to time.

At the level of state politics as well, one finds interesting tales of trust and mistrust between principal players in the events that have unfolded since 1947. Sheikh Mohammad Abdullah, Mirza Afzal Beg, Bakshi Ghulam Mohammad, G.M. Sadiq, Mir Qasim and D.P. Dhar were probably the best of colleagues, but their saga of friendship had its own trials and tribulations.

'FRIENDS' OF SHEIKH ABDULLAH

Of all the relationships between the people mentioned above, that of Sheikh Abdullah and Mirza Afzal Beg was a special one. It lasted for over fifty years. But the unceremonious ouster of Beg, the deputy chief minister in the Sheikh Abdullah cabinet in 1978, marked the parting of ways between Sheikh Abdullah and his legal eagle, Mirza Beg. On 18 October 1978, Beg blasted Sheikh Abdullah for his 'double talk'.[34] He brought to notice contradictions in the personality of Sheikh Abdullah. He asked people not to be swayed by the oratory of the chief minister, who he contended was in the habit of saying one thing in Srinagar, contradicting it in Jammu and then saying the same thing with a different meaning and connotation in New Delhi. This was obvious from the way the chief minister frequently stressed in the Valley that the Kashmir problem had not yet been solved, whereas in Jammu he stated that his reference was to 'Azad Kashmir' and in Delhi he conveyed in turn that by the Kashmir problem he meant the liberation of occupied areas of the state by Pakistan.

What was more revealing was that Beg charged that in 1965, when they had gone together along with Begum Abdullah to Medina, Sheikh Abdullah was reluctant to return to India after his passport had been cancelled by the Union Government. Begum Abdullah and he claimed to have argued with Sheikh Abdullah not to become an exile for the sake of hundreds of people who had sacrificed their lives after his arrest in 1953. Beg believed that Sheikh Abdullah was very critical of him, and when they were arrested on return to India and sent to Kodaikanal, he told the people of Kashmir that he would die fighting for their rights rather than live in exile. Perhaps Sheikh Abdullah had kept Beg in the dark about the likely developments in Kashmir due to a well-guarded strategy that only he was privy to. He did not seem to trust Beg implicitly.

On arrival from Jeddah in April 1965 after his hajj, Sheikh Abdullah was promptly arrested. Sheikh Abdullah had chosen to meet the Chinese premier, Zhou Enlai, in Algiers, at the Second Asian-African Conference. Relations between China and India were not good because China had inflicted heavy damage to India during the 1962 war. As it appears in the book *India, Pakistan and the Sacred Jihad: The Covert War in Kashmir (1947–2004)* by Praveen Swami,[35] there was a strongly held view that Abdullah knew that India and Pakistan would be at war. He quotes from Surendra Nath's report on Pakistan Organized Subversion that Sheikh Abdullah was sounded by Pakistani emissaries about Operation Gibraltar in 1965, which led to the Indo-Pak war.

Duane R. Clarridge in *A Spy for All Seasons: My Life in the CIA*,[36] reveals interesting incidents and the role of Sheikh Abdullah. Clarridge was a CIA agent who had a stint in India during 1960–64. He was advised that their headquarters had received information about regular Pakistani military units moving into Kashmir but they believed it would be irrational of Pakistan to do so.

So when and how did Sheikh Abdullah get in touch with Clarridge, a known spymaster? In 1964, after Jawaharlal Nehru released Sheikh Abdullah from prison, the latter immediately left for Paris. Clarridge flew to Paris to meet Sheikh Abdullah in a dingy hotel on the Left Bank. The CIA agent believed that Sheikh Abdullah probably thought that if it came to a face-off between the Indians and the Pakistanis, the United States (US) would side with Pakistan or at least stay out of it. The US was obviously a power involved in the Indo-Pakistan problem involving Kashmir. Pakistan, Turkey, Iran, Iraq and the United Kingdom were members of CENTO (The Central Treaty Organization), with the US as an observer. The US had its own military bases in Pakistan. The meeting was a bit tentative, though an agreement was reached to meet again in Jeddah, Saudi Arabia, where Sheikh Abdullah went for hajj.

Clarridge flew to Jeddah and contacted Abdullah, and this time was successful in extracting vital information from him. This information revolved around the events that would ultimately lead to the war between India and Pakistan in 1965.

Somehow Clarridge's report was ignored, as the CIA could not believe that the badly outstripped Pakistanis would really take on the Indian Army. They called upon him when the events unfolded as per his report, hence if there was anyone in Kashmir who knew about Operation Gibraltar much before anyone outside Pakistan, it was Sheikh Abdullah. How much of his involvement with the CIA regarding 1965 was known to the Government of India is unclear, but if Kashmiri leaders have failed to gain the trust of the leadership in Delhi, such incidents cannot be overlooked. Sheikh Abdullah, too, has been silent on meetings with Clarridge in his autobiography, though he mentions his meetings with Air Marshal Noor Khan and Pir Maqbool Gilani. According to him, Noor Khan did not drop even a hint at Pakistan being engaged in a move against India.[37]

Another comrade-in-arms of Sheikh Abdullah was Bakshi Ghulam Mohammad. Their excellent relationship and organizing ability as a team created a stir during the Quit Kashmir movement in 1931. But soon after working together in the cabinet for a couple of years, the two fell apart in 1953. Sheikh Abdullah believed that D.P. Dhar, G.M. Sadiq and all those he trusted conspired to throw him out of the office in 1953. Soon after his demise, his son Dr Farooq Abdullah and his son-in-law, Ghulam Mohammad Shah, too, fell apart.

There is a phrase in Kashmiri—waguv tsatun. Literally, waguv means a 'low-grade carpet' and tsatun means 'cutting'. It best describes the sinister moves by detractors to pull down anyone whose career is on an ascendance, a trait seen at all levels. What is surprising is that waguv tsatun is so common in most families, bureaucracies and politics—it is all-pervading. People believe it has become difficult to take Kashmiris at face value. This has complicated finding ways to resolve our problems. 'Except poplars, nothing is straight in Kashmir' is a quote often used to describe us. It was no wonder to hear that General K.V. Krishna Rao, who was the governor of J&K in 1993, while briefing the cabinet led by the prime minister P.V. Narasimha Rao asked if there was a Kashmiri sitting in the conference room during the confidential security briefing. He commented that Kashmiris were the most untrustworthy characters he had seen in his life. Little did he know that there was a Kashmiri sitting in the room!

On 21 July 2015, speaking at the release of the book *Kashmir: The Vajpayee Years* written by A.S. Dulat, Dr Farooq Abdullah mentioned, 'As I have always said, don't mistrust us, don't push us to the wall, we will die as Indians. I have always said that and I will continue to say that till I go to the grave and face my God.' Some months later, in an interview with *The Hindu* on 12 November 2015, he was candid. 'I did a lot and I did it to the best of my ability, but Delhi did not agree with me. The trust factor was missing right from my father's time.' They did not trust his father either.

And if one goes by what Farooq Abdullah seems to have confided in A.S. Dulat, Sheikh Abdullah was right in his assessment that his son may have to struggle to navigate his political career. 'I am not like father. I am not going to follow my father's politics. I do not intend to spend twenty-three years in jail. I have figured out that to remain in power here, you have to be on the right side of Delhi and that's what I am going to do,' Farooq Abdullah told A.S. Dulat.

Is politics so simple and straightforward for Kashmir? I wonder.

Lad Ded reminds us of the benefits of standing united:

Kyahkari paantsan dahan ti kahan
Vwakhshun yath lyejyi keryith gey
Seeryiy samihan yath razyi lamihan
Adi kyaazyi raavihye kahan gaav[38]

[With five, tens and elevens what shall I do?
All have thrust their hands into the pot;
Oh would all unite and pull the rope,
The cow belonging to eleven would have not gone astray.]

ENDNOTES

1   There is a wealth of written information on Kashmir, starting with
    Kalhana's *Rajatarangini* (*A Chronicle of the Kings of Kashmir*), translated
    by M.A. Stein. The three-volume work is a long narrative of events
    taking place in the Valley from the earliest times to AD 1150. Post
    Kalhana Pandit, four scholars have written sequels: Jonaraja (AD 1150-
    1459), Srivara Pandit (AD 1459-1486), Prajyabhatta (AD 1486-1512)
    and Suka (AD 1515-1586). Hence, Kashmir has a continuous history
    written in Sanskrit, till the acquisition by the Mughal king, Akbar, in
    AD 1587.

    In his book *A History of Kashmir*, P.N.K. Bamzai covers the
    political, social and cultural history of Kashmir from the earliest times
    to the 1960s. In the words of Jawaharlal Nehru, this book brings out a
    very special feature of our civilization—how Kashmir's mixed culture
    took shape. About 2,000 or more years ago, Kashmir was a centre of
    Buddhism; some of the famous Buddhist councils were held in Kashmir.
    Then Sanskrit flourished and it became the principal centre for the
    learning of Sanskrit. Nearly a thousand years ago, Arab and Persian
    influence came upon Kashmir. Later, under the Mughal rule, Persian
    became the official language. This has been a long story of sometimes

successively, sometimes simultaneously experiencing Buddhist, Hindu and Muslim influences, leading to a mixed but harmonized culture.

Another Kashmiri scholar and historian, Fida Mohammad Khan Hassanain, in his book *Historic Kashmir,* gives an excellent overview of the history and culture of Kashmir. It has essays on various aspects of our history and legacy that we can indeed be proud of. He emphasizes that the most precious heritage of the Kashmiris is their mixed culture; it is Shaivite, Buddhist and Islamic all at the same time.

Research and writings post-1947 have focussed on the legality of accession and the events emanating therefrom. The *Kashmir Dispute: 1947–2012* by A.G. Noorani is an encyclopaedia of events and commentaries. It has a chronological record of all that one needs to know about the accession of J&K to India, along with detailed explanation. *Jammu and Kashmir* by Jyoti Bhusan Dasgupta, while covering the internal dynamics of Kashmir, focusses on the international dimensions as well. It includes in detail the proceedings of the United Nations (UN) and resolutions of the Security Council. Published in 1967, it covers all the developments for resolving the dispute in a chronological order from 1947.

Distinguished former diplomat C. Dasgupta, in his book *War and Diplomacy in Kashmir (1947–48),* covered in depth the role played by Lord Mountbatten and the British Service Chief in India and Pakistan during the war in Kashmir in 1947–48. He has covered the roles played by western powers and China in the UN.

Rakesh Ankit in his book *The Kashmir Conflict: From Empire to the Cold War (1945–66)* has accessed declassified records that were closed for sixty-five years. He has seen files in the UK, the Commonwealth, the US and Russia. There is enough evidence emerging to place Kashmir in, as R.J. Moore put it, 'the revived *Great Game* in Asia' from 1947 itself, and probe its multiple phases.

Two books by Dr Manoj Joshi have indeed provided an excellent perception of contemporary events. *The Lost Rebellion: Kashmir in the Nineties* gives the reader all one requires to know about how the militant rebellion that began in Kashmir in the winter of 1989 and left over 20,000 dead was brought under control by the might of the Indian State. As the book claims, it is truly a riveting account of human drama that lies at the heart of the crisis that is Kashmir. His earlier book, *Kashmir 1947–1965: A Story Retold* brings out one point clearly that while the Indian case in Kashmir is strongly rooted in legality, there is profound emotion as well, which may not be visible at first sight but quickly comes to the fore when the issue of India's sovereignty is raised.

Prem Shankar Jha, an eminent journalist, in his book *Kashmir 1947: Rival Versions of History* writes on the contending opinions on the Kashmir issue at the time of Partition. We know the circumstances that made Maharaja Hari Singh seek accession to India. Pakistan has a version of events that disputes the Indian one.

Ambassador Husain Haqqani writes in his book *Reimagining Pakistan* that Pakistan no longer enjoys the support of the international community on the Kashmir issue. When the then prime minister Nawaz Sharif raised the Kashmir issue in the United Nations General Assembly in 2014, he was the only head of government to mention Kashmir out of 193 speakers. Yet, Pakistani leaders refuse to budge from their stance that Kashmir is the core issue in India-Pakistan relations. Ideology and pride come in the way of charting a sensible course.

Praveen Swami, a well-known expert on security studies, and author of *India, Pakistan and the Secret Jihad—The Covert War in Kashmir, 1947-2004*, has quoted extensively from the secret 'Report on Pakistani Organized Subversion, Sabotage and Infiltration in Jammu and Kashmir' by Surendra Nath, a senior police officer who steered India's counter-intelligence campaign against terrorist groups in J&K. The injecting of radicalism to change the dominant discourse of composite culture emerges as the greatest challenge facing Kashmiri society now.

A study on contemporary issues in Kashmir would be incomplete without mentioning Dr Karan Singh's *Heir Apparent* and *Autobiography*. Having been closely associated with post-accession events from 1947, it is a first-hand account of someone who has been there and seen it all. He was our first and last Sadr-i-Riyasat and first governor.

Based on her archival research, eminent scholar Chitralekha Zutshi has written an outstanding book titled *Languages of Belonging: Islam, Regional Identity, and the Making of Kashmir*. She has discussed Kashmiriyat as a historical entity and observed that it was, and continues to be, a series of dynamic identities that have emerged in interaction with, and at times been overshadowed by, other forms of belonging, particularly religious and national.

Basharat Peer, who was a teenager when the separatist movement exploded in Kashmir in 1989, has given an intimate account of the times through his own experience in the book *Curfewed Nights*. Rahul Pandita, who was 14 years old when he was forced to leave his home in Srinagar along with his family, too has captured the saga of a family in exile in his book *Our Moon Has Blood Clots: A Memoir of a Lost Home in Kashmir*. His book describes how Kashmiri Pandits were forced to leave their home and spend the rest of their lives in exile in their own country. Basharat Peer and Rahul Pandita have recorded for posterity the tragedy of our times.

Recently, Rakesh Kaul's bestselling fiction *The Last Queen of Kashmir* has brought alive Kota Rani, the last ruler queen of Kashmir of the fourteenth century, and has dealt at length as to how Islam set its roots in the Valley. Moreover, he has highlighted the higher goals of spirituality, the higher status of education and of women as the intrinsic bedrock of Kashmiri society.

2   Sing-a-Long, (2010, May 16). Hukus Bukus Telwan Tsukus—from

Mujtaba. http://www.koausa.org/muisc/shokachaniya/lyrics.html.

3   P.N.K. Bamzai, *A History of Kashmir: Political-Social-Cultural*, Srinagar: Gulshan Books, 2009. Kashmir was ruled by kings following Buddhist or Hindu/Vedic beliefs till the death of Kota Rani in 1339 AD. The Muslim rule of Shah Mir Dynasty lasted till 1586 when the last Chak ruler surrendered to the Mughal emperor Akbar. The Mughals governed Kashmir through various governors from 1587 to 1752 AD. Then came the Afghans who ruled from 1752 to 1819 AD, the Sikhs from 1819 to 1846 AD and the Dogras from 1846 to 1947 AD.

4   P.N.K. Bamzai, *A History of Kashmir: Political-Social-Cultural*, Srinagar: Gulshan Books, p 21, 2009.

5   Ibid, p 541

6   Ibid

7 Kashmiriyat is widely considered an extension of lihaaz, which means being tolerant and respectful of diverse narratives and people of different faiths.

8   Jawahar Lal Bhat, *Lal-Ded Revisited*. Vision Creative Services, 2014.

9   J.L.Kaul, 'Kashmiri Lyrics', Rinemisray, Srinagar, Kashmir, p. IX, 1945.

10   P.N.K. Bamzai, *A History of Kashmir: Political-Social-Cultural*, Srinagar: Gulshan Books, p 193, 2009.

11   https://www.encyclopedia.com/places/asia/indian-political-geography/jammu-and-kashmir

12   Arabinda Basu and Aanadi Pal, Human Remains from Burzahom, Anthropological Society of India, p 3, March 1980.

13   P.N.K. Bamzai, *A History of Kashmir: Political-Social-Cultural*, Srinagar: Gulshan Books, p 153, 2009.

14   Ibid, pp 168-170.

15   Project 'ZAAN' – Information Digest, Vol. 1, March 2001.

16   Walter R. Lawrence, *The Valley of Kashmir*. Srinagar: Gulshan Books, 2011.

17   A.S. Dulat and Aditya Sinha, *Kashmir: The Vajpayee Years*. New Delhi: Harper Collins Publishers India, 2015.

18   V.S. Naipaul, *An Area of Darkness: His Discovery of India*, New Delhi: Picador India, pp 105–127, 2010.

19   Walter R. Lawrence, *The Valley of Kashmir*. Srinagar: Gulshan Books, 2011.

20   Sheikh Mohammad Abdullah, *The Blazing Chinar: An Autobiography*. Srinagar: Gulshan Books, p 24, 2013.

21   Ramesh Kumar, (May 2003) 'Allama Iqbal—Searching for Pandit Roots', *Kashmir Sentinel*, http://www.panunkashmir.org

22   Sheikh Mohammad Abdullah, *The Blazing Chinar: An Autobiography*, Srinagar: Gulshan Books, p 57, 2013.

23   G. Allana, 'Two Letters from Iqbal to Jinnah (1937)'. *Pakistan Movement Historical Documents*, Karachi: Department of International Relations, University of Karachi, pp 129–133, 1969.

24   www.suhaillaripakistan.com/chapters/Lahore

25   'Iqbal's Hindu Relations', *The Telegraph*, 30 June 2007.

26   G. Allana, *Pakistan Movement Historical Documents*, Karachi Department of International Relations, University of Karachi, pp. 103–110, 1969.

27   Ibid, pp 103–110.

28   Mohammad Ali Jinnah, 'Presidential Address at Lahore Session of the Muslim League', March 1940, *Directorate of Films and Publishing, Ministry of Information and Broadcasting*, Government of Pakistan, Islamabad, pp 5–23, 1983.

29   Sheikh Mohammad Abdullah, *The Blazing Chinar*, Srinagar: Gulshan Books, 2013.

30   Kalhana, *Rajtarangini: A Chronicle of the Kings of Kashmir*. Vol. 1, Srinagar: Gulshan Books, p 9, 2007.

31   Sheikh Mohammad Abdullah, *The Blazing Chinar*, Srinagar: Gulshan Books, 2013.

32 'Relief in Kashmir as Prophet's Relic is Recovered', *The Times of India*, 5 January 1964.

33 Inder Malhotra, 'Hanging by a Hair', *The Indian Express*, 9 August 2010.

34 Beg Blasts Sheikh for 'double-talk', *The Times of India*, 9 October 1978.

35 Praveen Swami, India, Pakistan and The Secret Jihad: The Covert War in Kashmir, 1947-2004, Routledge, 2006.

36 Duane R. Clarridge, *A Spy for All Seasons*. New York: Scribner, pp 103-105, 1997.

37 Sheikh Mohammad Abdullah, *The Blazing Chinar*, Srinagar: Gulshan Books, p 513, 2013.

38 Jawahar Lal Bhat, *Lal-Ded Revisited*, Vision Creative Services, pp 144, 2014.

PART 2
TRAVELOGUE

7

KASHMIR TO KUMAON

Like most Kashmiris, I had not crossed the Banihal tunnel, which connected the Valley with the outside world until 1966. And what I saw helped shape my life. Likewise, I believe it did so for many of my friends who, too, left with me to study in Nainital.

I was amongst some twenty-five students from J&K selected by the government to study in Sainik School, Ghorakhal, Nainital (SSGK). Ours was the first and last batch of students from J&K to study in SSGK. A Sainik School came up in Nagrota, Jammu, later, hence the government of J&K stopped sponsoring students to study in schools outside the state.

My first interview in life was for admission to Ghorakhal with Wing Commander Jaimal Singh, Principal, who had come for the final selections to Srinagar. He interviewed all the shortlisted candidates in the Civil Secretariat building of Srinagar. As much as I was excited about taking the first interview of my life (I was 11 years old), I was equally happy to visit the Civil Secretariat, as to the best of my recollection, it was the only building in Kashmir which was fitted with a lift. As to how many times I went up and down in the lift, I cannot recall, but it was enough to get a reprimand from the liftman, asking me to allow officegoers to use the lift.

AT HOME IN THE HILLS

I often call Kumaon my second home. The Indo-China War of 1962 and the Indo-Pak War of 1965 had exposed me as a child growing up in Kashmir to army bunkers in parks and the movement of heavy armoury and tanks. Our neighbour in Jawahar Nagar, Srinagar, was a young army captain. If there was any ambition I harboured in 1965, it was to become an army captain like him and join the infantry. On knowing that the state government was sending students to Ghorakhal, Nainital, for eventual entry to the National Defence Academy (NDA), my father and tutor advised me to seek admission and use this route to become an army officer.

While most of us were from the Kashmir Valley, there were students from Jammu and Ladakh as well. My first thought on reaching Ghorakhal in August 1966 was that I was not going to miss the Kashmir Valley, as the hills of Kumaon welcomed us with open arms. The journey to Ghorakhal was also my first train travel from Pathankot.

Sainik School, Ghorakhal, near Nainital, was established on 21 March 1966 on the magnificent estate of the Nawab of Rampur. The name Ghorakhal relates to the events in 1857, when a British general, in a desperate bid to escape the revolutionaries of Awadh, strayed into this area, and his horse, while drinking water from a nearby pond, died. Therefore the name ghora (horse) khal (pond). The Ghorakhal estate was presented to General Wheeler in 1870 by the British rulers. In 1921, the then nawab of Rampur, Sir Syed Mohammad Hamid Ali Khan Bahadur, purchased this estate. After the abolition of the privy purses in post-Independence India, the state government (then Uttar Pradesh) purchased the estate from the Nawab of Rampur in March 1964, and Sainik School, Ghorakhal, was established on 21 March 1966. The famous Hindi movie, *Madhumati,* starring Dilip Kumar, my favourite actor, and Vyjayanthimala, was shot in and around this school.

Before joining Sainik School, Ghorakhal, I had studied in Ganpatyar School and DAV School in Srinagar. While I passed the UPSC written examination for admission to the NDA, I could not stand the physical rigour of the tests by the Service Selection Board (SSB), Jabalpur. I still remember how dejected I felt on that day, not knowing what to do next. It was Ian Jarry, Graduate Volunteer Service Overseas (GVSO), who had come from the UK to teach in our school, who counselled me in choosing a career. He introduced me to the world of Chemical Engineering based on my aptitude and interests in case I was not selected for the NDA again. By a strange coincidence, other Kashmiri Ghorakhalians who qualified in the Union Public Service Commission (UPSC) written exams, too, were rejected by the Service Selection Board (SSB) or during medical tests, and did not join the NDA.

It was so heartening to learn that a young boy, Ummer Fayaz, after studying in a local army school in the Valley, had joined the NDA and later the Indian Military Academy (IMA) and become a commissioned officer in December 2016. He had succeeded in clearing the SSB and medical tests, which we had failed forty-five years back. Alas, he was killed by militants in a dastardly act when he was attending the marriage of his sister in Shopian in May 2017, at the young age of 22. Being a direct recruit of NDA/ IMA, with age on his side, Ummer could have definitely aimed to be the first Kashmiri Muslim to become one of the heads of the Indian Armed Forces and surpassed the existing distinction held by Major General Amin Naik (Retd). Hope his demise does nothing to demotivate aspirations of other teenagers to join the state or central defence forces.

After leaving Ghorakhal, I studied in NIT Srinagar, and IIT Kanpur. But if there is any institution that can take the credit for laying the foundation for everything many of us students from J&K have achieved in our lives, it would justifiably be Sainik School, Ghorakhal, rated now amongst the top fifteen boarding schools for boys in India by an independent rating agency. Two students of our batch joined the IAS, five became doctors, two joined the defense services, two became engineers and the rest did well in their respective chosen professions.

My late friend, Mohammad Iqbal Khanday, IAS, who retired as chief secretary, J&K, was the first IAS officer from the state to become chief secretary. Khurshid Ahmad Ganai, IAS, who serves as advisor to the governor of J&K, and former chief information commissioner, Dr J.P. Singh, a well-known neurosurgeon, are fellow Ghorakhalians.

It was gratifying to see students from my school emerge with flying colours and create examples for others to follow in the state.

Access to employable holistic education is the need of the hour for our future generations as they enter a world of uncertainty, volatility, complexity and ambiguity. If the foundation of education is of high quality, there is no reason why students from Kashmir will not do well in their lives. I realize what access to quality schooling can do to Kashmiris who study in J&K or outside. Making education available freely is a job only half done if it does not promote holistic learning. Education gave us a window to the outside world to see what others thought of Kashmiris and how and whether at all we were different in any way from people of the other Indian states.

Our school had students from many states, including the north-east. It gave us the first experience of how warmly teachers and students outside J&K treated us. Without exaggerating, I must confess that students from Kashmir received enormous love and were given special coaching to bring them on a par with other students. Sometimes I found the treatment too special, much to the disdain of others, but none protested, though there was uniformity and discipline for all students.

While we got along well with people of all regions, our bonding with students from Kumaon and the north-east was special. Was there a sublime connection between children of the hills, from Kashmir to Kumaon to Khasi? One of the reasons for the backwardness of the hills as compared to the plains prompted protests in Kumaon, leading to the creation of Uttarakhand. Gorkhaland remains troubled. Kashmir, too, remains insulated from the plains. Our stories are similar in some ways.

It was also the first time that I realized that while we had apprehensions about living in a distant land, not many people were aware of the status of Kashmir as an independent kingdom at the time of India's Independence. Questions were always asked about the loyalty of Kashmiris, but in a friendly way. There were some doubting Thomases, and religious affiliation provided no support in difficult times. If Kashmiris were not integrated within India, it was not that much integration had happened the other way round either.

8

PAKISTAN
(Safar Apour)

Ever since childhood, I have sensed a strange curiosity among Kashmiris for Pakistan. This could be either because the Valley is predominantly Muslim and there is a religious affinity with the neighbouring country, or because a major part of disputed J&K is in Pakistan. No wonder that so many times apour would get discussed.

Apour in Kashmiri language means next room or neighbour. But when two Kashmiris talk about a third person having gone apour in hushed tones, it means the person has crossed the border and travelled illegally to Pakistan.

My first visit to Pakistan in 1998 was for a personal reason. I was working with the Al-Dabbagh Group of Saudi Arabia, led by Sheikh Amr Al-Dabbagh, who later also served as Chairman of SAGIA (Saudi Arabian General Investment Authority). I was vice president of the Al-Dabbagh Group of companies in the Energy portfolio. My immediate superior, Akhtar Zaidi, executive vice president and chief operating officer, was an American citizen of

Pakistani origin. He was getting married in Karachi to Gul, an in-flight staff with Emirates airlines, and invited members of the executive team to attend his wedding reception. Other members of the team, David Retallack and John Parry, were citizens of the UK and had no visa issues in travelling to Pakistan. Being an Indian passport holder and a state subject of J&K, I had my own apprehensions about whether the Jeddah consulate of Pakistan would grant me a travel visa at such short notice.

Akhtarbhai felt otherwise. He called someone at the consulate and told them that I was like his brother and my stay in Karachi would not be for more than two days. After this, I went to the consulate office of Pakistan in Jeddah with my passport and other papers as required, and to my surprise, my visa was approved in less than an hour! I could not believe it. Perhaps the fact that Akhtarbhai, one of the highly ranked investment bankers and management professionals, was my guarantor had helped expedite the matter.

Excited to attend a Pakistani wedding, I took an Emirates flight from Dubai to Karachi, along with David, John and Walid Akawi, a colleague who worked in the publishing business of Al-Dabbagh in Dubai. The Karachi airport in 1998 was miles ahead of Indian airports—modern and well-regulated. After passing the immigration, I saw someone handing over a form to people for police verification for Indian passport holders. I, too, collected a form but my other colleagues had no need for it. We all were booked in Karachi Marriott Hotel. As soon as we checked in, I told the hotel manager in front of all my colleagues that since I was an Indian passport holder, he should send my passport for police verification.

'Sir, you are staying for only one night. There is no need for police verification for you,' he replied.

'I arrived in the afternoon and am leaving tomorrow by a late-night flight. Hence I shall be staying in Karachi for more than twenty-four hours. Technically for about thirty-six hours. So please, get my police verification done,' I requested.

'You are technically right, sir. But with Nawaz Sharif and Vajpayee ji at the helm, our relations have improved. If you were to stay for two nights, we would do it. Do not worry, sir. We will take care of it. You can keep your passport with you,' he said in a reassuring voice.

My colleagues who were witness to the conversation felt that we should go by the advice of Marriott, as they must be well versed with tourism laws, and left it at that.

Akhtarbhai had drawn up an excellent itinerary for all of us. I was picked up by his friend and taken to Karachi Gymkhana for lunch. The Gymkhana, founded in 1886, was one of the largest clubs in Asia in view of its membership and sports facilities. It was a pleasure to take a short trip of the facilities. A big banner announcing 'Yoga Classes for Women' caught my attention.

Settling at the lunch table, I enquired of my host as to how women in Karachi had developed interest in yoga. The conversation that followed was suddenly disrupted by a noisy discussion amongst a group of middle-aged people seated a couple of tables away.

'What is happening on that table? It seems they will fight,' I told my host.

'Don't worry, Ashokji. These buggers have a leader sitting in London and will never learn how to behave in a club,' he answered.

'Who in London?' I asked.

'Ah! Their guardian, who does not have the guts to come to Karachi. His name is Altaf Hussain. He heads the Muhajir

Qaumi Movement (MQM). But these muhajirs will always remain second-class citizens,' he responded.

I could see my host hailed from original West Pakistan and did not hold muhajirs in high esteem. MQM comprises largely of Urdu-speaking Muslims who migrated from India to Pakistan after Partition; it has a strong presence in Karachi and is now the largest party in Sindh with a significant presence overall as well.

Having started our lunch, I settled down to ask my learned host a couple of questions on Kashmir.

'Tell me, how do you explain your love for Kashmiris if people who migrated here in 1947 are still second-class citizens?' I asked.

'What love for Kashmiris? They are living in a fool's paradise. Frankly speaking, they will be third-class citizens in Pakistan. My friend, we all know Kashmiri women are beautiful. We will marry them. The men will work for us as our employees, as all business will be in our hands,' he said plainly.

'Sadly, Kashmiri Muslims do not realize this possibility. Some of them may believe co-religionists in Pakistan may provide them a better future,' I responded.

'It is their destiny. Who is worried about people? We want access to water. Punjab and Sindh must continue to get water from the rivers of Kashmir. Imagine if water stops flowing to us, what will become of Pakistan,' he clarified with a deep understanding of drivers of Pakistan interest in Kashmir.

'Interesting! Your analysis may be right, but the Indus Water Treaty has been held up well. I agree, Kashmiris are living in a fool's paradise.'

Looking back, I realize how deep my friend's insight was, for Verghese Koithara, in his book *Crafting Peace in Kashmir: Through a Realist Lens*,[1] has observed that to both India and Pakistan, J&K

appeared to be a prize at the time of Partition, especially from the perspective of territory, deterrence and resources. And most importantly, the matter of rivers—the Indus, the Jhelum and the Chenab flow out of the state.

I wondered why we in Kashmir do not understand that perception of a brotherhood on the basis of religion is an illusion. If it were so, Arab countries in the Gulf would have been one nation. My host was not sugar-coating his words—he said what he believed in and my later interactions made me feel that there was little in common culturally, socially and linguistically between Kashmiris and Muslims in Pakistan.

AN UNEXPECTED ADVENTURE

After lunch, on arrival at the Karachi Marriott, David and John were waiting for us to take a tour of the city. Karachi has a rich cultural history. Before the Partition of India, it had a mixed population, but now it is predominantly Muslims— Sunnis comprising almost two-third and Shias one-third of the population. On reaching the main market, we decided to take a buggy ride—a ride on a horse-driven carriage—and go around the main bazaar. All eyes were on my two European friends, and we wondered if the Taliban would not have an easy target of these visitors in the commercial and financial hub of Pakistan. Luckily, we all returned to the hotel safe, with a good experience of the buggy ride, and got ready to attend the dinner reception at Akhtarbhai's residence in the posh Civil Lines area.

It was a reception no different from the receptions of the rich and famous in India. Ladies in their best attire, men smoking and drinking (alcohol, despite the Sharia ban), and Bollywood music being played by the DJ at as high a pitch and volume as we did in India. It was as good as being in Delhi attending any typical Punjabi wedding reception.

However, there was a twist. After about half an hour of having settled down, all music stopped and a professional master of ceremonies took the floor and introduced a troupe from Lahore, which was to perform a number of kathak items. What followed for the next couple of hours was a treat to watch. Perfect Sanskrit recitation, perfect kathak dance moves and an appreciative audience. I just could not believe my eyes that after seeing 'Yoga for Women' at the Gymkhana, I was witnessing one of the best kathak dance recitals in my life in Pakistan. India had so much in common with Pakistan. Partition had not broken the cultural bonds—Indians relished the same food, wore the same dresses and enjoyed similar music and dance. The programme went on late into the night as the kathak recital was followed by local dances and a mujra. With appreciation being showered through currency notes on dancers, I, too, was handed a bundle of Pakistani notes by Ghazzanfar Awam, another colleague at Dabbagh, and had the honour of showering the same on dancers through midnight!

Next day, Akhtarbhai invited all of us to lunch at a picnic spot in the city, and we all reached the hotel in time to take some rest before embarking on our return flight. We checked in at the airport and went to the immigration desk. While David, John and Waleed were allowed past immigration, I was stopped. My friends joined me in asking immigration the reason and, to my surprise, it was the police verification that had cause the problem. We told the immigration officer what had transpired at the check-in counter at the Marriott and how the manager had reassured us that police verification would not be required for me since I was staying for only one night in Karachi.

But the immigration officer would accept none of it and allowed others to go, but asked me to follow him to the head of immigration at Karachi airport. All my excitement and positive energy had vanished by now.

By now Akhtarbhai had received news of my predicament and called me on my cell phone. His call was reassuring because I had at least one local person of some standing as support. I told him that I was on the way to the office of the Head of Immigration, and described what had happened.

The head of immigration was a nice man, as he did everything to make me feel comfortable. I narrated what had happened, and he called up the hotel manager of Marriott and their local representative at the airport. The hotel manager corroborated my version.

Suddenly, someone rushed in from outside to the head's room and demanded the passport of 'the Indian who was to embark on an Emirates flight to Dubai'. The head of immigration looked up and without saying a word to me, left, along with my passport.

My eyes were fixed on the hall outside, and through the glass wall I saw the head of immigration showing my passport to a person dressed in a greyish safari suit who seemed to be a superior officer, as about a dozen people were standing by him at attention. He saw my passport and returned it to the head, who handed it to his subordinate. Soon, this person came running to me with my passport and asked me to rush to catch the flight.

I gathered all the energy I had left and raced to board the plane. Passengers, on seeing me, gave me nasty looks; but David, John and Waleed were happy to see me back.

'What just happened?' asked David.

'Nothing, David. Let me sleep. What just happened was because of the different passports we hold.'

Thus, my first visit apour was one I cannot forget, both for the excellent hospitality of Akhtarbhai and the exit experience at Karachi airport.

SOUNDS AND SIGHTS

I returned to India from the Middle East and joined the petroleum business of Reliance Industries Ltd. in May 2001. Having been associated with the oil industry for long and being a regular speaker at national and international conferences, I was not surprised when the Petroleum Institute of Pakistan, Islamabad, invited me to address the Oil & Gas Conference 2007 in Islamabad.

Despite my experience on my previous visit, I again travelled without police verification. Even with my not-so-happy memories, while entering Karachi city from the airport, I was excited. I would be attending the international conference, and sharing my knowledge and gaining an overview of the oil and gas industry in Pakistan. I was equally keen to understand why Pakistan was reluctant to import petroleum products directly from India to meet its deficit.

The theme for my talk was 'Preparing for meeting Asia's fuel requirement'. The hospitality of the hosts was commendable. We had a free Sunday and my friend, Mir, my business associate, who represented Reliance for some petrochemical products, invited me to have lunch at Kashmira restaurant at Daman-e-Koh, Islamabad.

One gets a mesmerizing view of Islamabad from Daman-e-Koh. It is like having a view of our Valley from Shankaracharya hills. Islamabad is one of the cleanest cities I have seen in South Asia. Kashmira restaurant assumed fame after Benazir Bhutto and Rajiv Gandhi met over tea here. And it was my turn now to have lunch at the same place.

As soon as I entered the restaurant, my attention was drawn towards some photos pinned at the gate by the owner. The photos were of some Hurriyat leaders from Kashmir who had visited Pakistan sometime earlier. I could identify some of them and felt joyous that I would be enjoying Kashmiri wazwan in Islamabad here at Kashmira restaurant.

It was quite natural for me to order Kashmiri wazwan and Mir too looked forward to relish the same. I fondly recall having kebabs and gushtaba at Ahdoo's restaurant in Srinagar and looked forward to a sumptuous Kashmiri meal here till the menu card was kept before us. There was not a single Kashmiri cuisine item on the menu, and my host who had invited me to the best Kashmiri restaurant in Islamabad was seemingly embarrassed. He called for the manager and the chief chef. Both confirmed their inability to make gushtaba or rista, or any of the Kashmiri dishes that I wished to have. Both said these were special Kashmiri dishes made on select occasions by a cook who came from Mirpur. That is what they had done when leaders of the Hurriyat had visited.

On 6 September 2008, Asif Ali Zardari, husband of late Benazir Bhutto, was elected as the president of Pakistan by the electoral college and he, too, made symbolic gestures at improving bilateral relations between India and Pakistan.

Towards the later part of his innings, he visited India in April 2012. Though it was a private visit to Ajmer Sharif, he did meet Dr Manmohan Singh, the prime minister of India, over lunch on 5 April. It was the first visit of a Pakistani head of state to India since 2005, and the primary concern was terrorism, due to the 2008 Mumbai attacks. A peace dialogue between India and Pakistan, suspended after the 2008 attacks, had resumed in February 2011.

It is said that at this meeting, Zardari asked Dr Singh to help Pakistan meet its deficit in the energy sector, both in power and hydrocarbons. To take this forward, the Government of India, under the aegis of the Ministry of Petroleum and National Gas, deputed a delegation of the oil industry to Islamabad in May 2012, of which I was a member.

UNDER THE SPELL OF THE US

This time again, as the visit was official, no police verification was required. We boarded the Pakistan International Airlines (PIA) flight from New Delhi to Lahore, from where we took the connecting flight to Islamabad on the evening of 26 May 2012. I had a chance encounter with someone whom I had seen many times on Indian and foreign TV channels but never imagined I would meet in real life. He was saying his travel prayers, or dua.

When leaving for a trip, whether for personal or official work, and undertaking any kind of travel, Muslims say a prayer to honour Allah and ask Him to protect them in the journey.

Looking at my co-passenger again, who had almost finished counting his beads to recite his prayer, I wondered where I had seen him before. He looked so familiar. As soon as he had finished and settled for the plane to take off, as if in a flash, I remembered. I was sitting next to General Hamid Gul, a familiar face on Indian television, espousing the case of the Taliban and such others.

It was a small plane, probably a forty-seater. I was on the aisle seat and he had taken the window. I turned politely to engage his attention and said, 'Salaam Alaykum. If I am not wrong, you must be General Gul.'

'Yes, I am.'

'I have seen you many times on Indian TV channels.'

'But I think you do not like what I say.'

'People do listen to your views. In any case, dialogue is necessary.'

I introduced myself. Then he resumed.

'Dhar sahib, so what brings you to Pakistan?'

'I am a member of a trade delegation from India visiting Islamabad.'

'Have a good time but do not waste time on trade. *Kuch nahi hone wala hai jab tak asli Kashmir ka masla hal nahin hota.*' (Nothing is going to happen till the Kashmir issue is resolved.)

'Trade is good. People meet people, and for resolving disputes, definitely dialogue is the way forward. Incidentally, I am a Kashmiri Pandit and we were driven out of the Valley during the turmoil. We lost our home and hearth, but we believe that we will return with honour and dignity, one day, Inshallah.'

'You must become independent.'

'How can we survive as an independent Kashmir? Who other than Pakistan will recognize an independent Kashmir?'

'Let me tell you that the first country to recognize independent Kashmir after us shall be the US.'

'What, the US? I thought they wanted India and Pakistan to resolve all disputes bilaterally. That is what I read in the media. General Musharraf...'

'Don't talk about Musharraf. He is a shame. He is the biggest mistake of my life. I promoted him. People who have a peculiar gait, with drooping shoulders, are untrustworthy. Also, you have never understood the US. I know them in and out.

It took us decades to realize who they are. Indians are now under their spell. I have been to their strategic conferences and can tell you for sure that they will always support an independent Kashmir. We have to realize that western models are not applicable everywhere and will not work in our part of the world. I was told to dissuade the Taliban from fighting the US after September 2001. I addressed a large group of Taliban fundamentalists for a couple of hours. I kept describing the deadly high-tech arsenal available with the US to the group of warlords. I told them in detail about the havoc modern weapons could create. There was pin-drop silence in the room. I thought to myself that they had probably understood the threat, until their leader got up to ask, 'You know Russians had equally big tanks and also what we did to them. They had to retreat and leave their armaments for us. All I want to ask you is what would be the strategy of Americans—will they leave this high-tech equipment with us after we defeat them?'

'Ha ha ha. That is very interesting.'

My friend, Ramgardhia, from Petrofed, sitting on my left, was getting scared at my loud laugh.

'The point is simple. No one has ever defeated the Afghans. They have a different model of governance. Why impose the western model of democracy on them?'

I managed to change the topic.

'It seems the plane is about to land now. It was indeed a pleasure to speak to you in person.'

'Yes, it is a short flight. Have a good time in Islamabad. Enjoy your stay.'

As we were deplaning, I saw a group of senior staff at the airport receiving General Gul and wondered at the chance encounter it had been with one of the ideologues of radical Islam in South Asia. When I shared the gist of my conversation with a former minister and a senior senator at the Pakistan National Assembly, both felt Pakistan would have avoided radical Islam but for General Gul, and wished I had had a chance encounter with a sane Pakistani and not him!

Now General Gul is no more, and I hope he rests in peace. He did come across as a highly conservative idealist who had perhaps understood the American strategy in South Asia in great depth and seen the good, the bad and the ugly side of global politics.

On my return, I was invited by ORF Delhi to give a talk on my visits to Pakistan. ORF is a leading independent think tank in India that emerged in the 1990s, in the wake of liberalization and an emerging global economic world order. Since then, it has been active in aiding policy formulation and providing well-researched analyses and inputs to decision-makers in the government, business communities, academics and civil society groups. I have been fortunate to be associated with this leading think tank since 2007, first as a distinguished fellow (primarily focussing on the energy sector, hydrocarbons in particular), and now helping it set up a branch of global excellence in Kolkata.

My talks on my impressions of Pakistan from my visits were attended, amongst others, by senior policy thinkers and one of the country's leading journalists who specialized in international relations. I shared my impressions from 1998, 2007 and 2012, emphasizing on the similarity of culture, dress, language and common aspirations. However, I also talked about how many felt that the terms of Partition had been unfair. Their institutions and bureaucracy lacked the maturity and depth of India. They feel that they hadn't got a fair share of resources. They wanted to catch up by strengthening democratic institutions, but the narrative had been clouded after the Islamization step by Zia-ul-Haq.

I remembered what General Gul had said about the US being the first country to recognize an independent Kashmir after Pakistan. And he was not wrong. The international relations experts I spoke with in India seemed to agree on the US's ambiguous and self-vested views on Kashmir. I recounted this to a senior secretary working for the government, an experienced journalist in international affairs, a senior ex-intelligence services officer and a retired general, asking their views on this, and they were all of the opinion that General Gul might have been right.

The impressions I gathered from my three brief travels apour were that the grass was not greener on the other side. The Almighty had given Kashmir all that He could have. But it was up to us to preserve our paradise and build our own path to livelihood, happiness and prosperity. Regrettably, Kashmir had been used by politicians in Pakistan to arouse passions for a cause that helped them keep their country united. As Sumit Ganguly writes, 'Kashmir is Pakistan's irredenta.'[2] They will have to figure out a different national narrative to survive as a united nation, and we will have to help ourselves chalk out our path for a modern, secular, progressive, peaceful and prosperous Kashmir.

Kashmir may remain Pakistan's irredenta as long as it does not find a new narrative to survive and remain united. The Pakistan of today is the Islamic Republic of Pakistan as nurtured by General Zia. It is not the Pakistan of Jinnah—a Muslim majority, democratic, liberal and secular nation. While there are people with liberal and secular values who want amity with India, I had found increasingly deep societal fissures in Pakistan on my last two visits.

These differences were of the following kind—mohajir versus

non-mohajir, Sunni versus Shia, Ahmadiyya versus the rest, Pashtun versus non-Pashtun, and so on. Ideological differences on the basis of the nation state's need for access to water resources, the presence of radical elements and the hold of militancy on statecraft emerged as key takeaways, rather than real love for Kashmir and Kashmiris. Sadly, I could not see the image or shades of our Kashmiriyat in Pakistan.

9

GLOBAL PERCEPTIONS

From 1992 to 2000, I travelled to many countries for professional duties. Most of the countries that exported crude oil to India were Islamic nations. So every time I got to interact with them or visit them, it was natural for me to compare Kashmir to them. I have visited Saudi Arabia, Iran, Kuwait, Yemen, Syria, the UAE, Oman, Bahrain, Qatar, Jordon, Lebanon, Libya and Sudan. I have interacted with people from Egypt, Malaysia, Indonesia and other Muslim countries, including Pakistan and Bangladesh.

SWITZERLAND—THE KASHMIR OF EUROPE

Kashmir has often been compared with Switzerland in terms of its natural beauty. What is lesser known is the fact that like Kashmir, which is inhabited by three distinct ethno-religious groups—Hindus, Muslims and Buddhists—Switzerland, too, has three ethnic groups that speak different languages. Many feel that the Swiss model could serve as a benchmark for Kashmir in moving towards a durable political solution. While returning from a training programme in London in 1993, I had a stopover at Geneva. The prospect of visiting Switzerland had always excited me, as I was accustomed to hearing Kashmir being compared with Switzerland since my childhood days.

As I dreamily gazed at the picturesque Lake Geneva from the balcony of my hotel room, I was transported to Srinagar, on the banks of the Dal Lake. I marvelled at the fountain at the centre of the lake but, biased as I was, I secretly derived joy from the feeling that Kashmir was far more beautiful than Switzerland. Instantly, I felt that the saying 'Kashmir is the Switzerland of the East' should be reversed to 'Switzerland is the Kashmir of Europe'. I read about how Switzerland had evolved into a peaceful country from the shambles of ethnic strife and wished Kashmir would evolve in a similar way. Despite the early history of Switzerland being marked by frequent invasions and ethnic clashes amongst the local population, from the mid-nineteenth century, order was restored, in the region followed by a long epoch of political stability and rapid industrial growth.

Switzerland is a melting pot of three distinct cultures: Italian, German and French. It was once an integral part of the holy Roman Empire. After the fall of the Roman Empire, it was invaded by Germanic tribes. Eventually, Switzerland was brought under French control by Napoleon in 1798, who transformed it into an ally known as the Helvetic Republic (1798–1803). Napoleon dismantled the existing federal political structure of Switzerland and transformed it into a centrally governed unitary state. It was only after the Congress of Vienna (1814–1815) that independence was restored in the country. The Congress of Vienna ushered in momentous changes in the history of Switzerland. It not only re-established the old confederation of sovereign states but also accorded the status of permanent armed neutrality to Switzerland in international law. Further, in 1848, following a brief civil war between Protestants and Catholics, Switzerland adopted a federal constitution. The attempt of the Catholic cantons to break away from the country was crushed, resulting in the formation of a stronger federal structure.

The constitution was further amended in 1874 and ensured greater autonomy for the cantons. Since then, the Swiss cantons have remained powerful bodies, each having its own distinctive structure and policies while also retaining its unique ethnic characteristics. This has not only ensured peaceful co-existence of the three principal ethnic groups—the Italians, the French and the German—but has also facilitated political stability and faster economic growth in the region.

Why only Switzerland? No other western country has ever surrendered its territorial sovereignty. Like Switzerland, the constitutions of France and Germany are also predicated on the sanctity of territorial sovereignty, more cogently on the notion that once a nation is formed, it cannot be undone. Similarly, the American Civil War affirmed the irrevocability of the federal government in the various states of America. The federal structure has also been upheld in Australia. Experts I spoke to confirmed that the Supreme Court of the US ruled that states cannot secede from the union, in the Texas versus White case in 1869. Similarly, the Australian constitution describes the federation as 'one indissoluble federal commonwealth'. If territorial sovereignty is sacrosanct, non-negotiable and irrevocable for the western nations, why shouldn't that be the case for India in deciding the fate of Kashmir?

But whether we can emulate the Swiss model needs to be examined and weighed against our ability to remain neutral. Kashmir participates in protests against incidents in the Islamic world either as a natural response to injustice or because it is easily used by vested groups even when leading Islamic nations like Saudi Arabia or Iran remain silent. While it is understandable and justifiable to protest against excesses in Gaza, to express solidarity with Palestine, such protests in the Valley tend to turn violent leading to the loss of precious lives.[3] Switzerland has remained neutral in the most troubling and demanding international conflicts. Can we remain so even when provoked?

ISLAM IN SAUDI ARABIA

Most countries that I visited, apart from Switzerland and others in the west, which exported crude oil to India, were Islamic nations.

Towards the end of 1995, I landed an assignment in Saudi Arabia which gave me enough time and opportunity to feel the differences first-hand. I travelled for business to most countries in the Middle East and also lived in Dubai for over a year as part of my contract with my employer.

While in Jeddah, I was part of a group of Kashmiris. Dr Manzoor Qazi, Zaffar Lone, Sanjay Sadhu, Vinay Fotedar, a few others and I used to meet almost every week to share Kashmiri delicacies. We lamented about what was happening to our home state and always prayed for Kashmiriyat to win in the end.

Saudi Arabia, the UAE and Iran were three countries I travelled to frequently from 1996 to 1999, and found more similarities in our value system with Sufi Islam as emanating from the Central Asian region like Iran than with most other nations. Saudis used to make no secret of their plan to expand the reach of Wahhabi Islam and deploy financial muscle to help propagate Wahhabism to win over poorer states. Announcements in recent years by Crown Prince Mohammad bin Salman do show promise of a policy change for propogation of a more moderate face of Islam. Time alone will tell how such pronouncements will be implemented in coming times.

Kashmir, on the contrary, has had a different foundation for Islam. One thing has always struck me. We in Kashmir are different. This is probably because our forefathers assimilated the essence of all religions and evolved a composite culture. Islam as practised in Kashmir has many visible differences.

Many Muslim countries in the Middle East do not understand the contours of the problem in Kashmir. They get influenced largely by reports of human rights violation—some right, some exaggerated. In 1994, things indeed reached a crescendo and attracted the attention of the UN Human Rights Convention at Geneva. PM Narasimha Rao picked a great team, with Vajpayee as the leader and Salman Khurshid as a member of the Indian delegation. Team India delivered and secured a reprieve. I visited Tehran as a member of the government-led delegation to finalize the terms of contract to import crude oil in 1993. I recall a dinner hosted at Sindbad restaurant by Dr Ghanimi Fard, the deputy minister for international trade in Iran and head of international business, and one of the foremost experts in the oil sector in Iran. Iran had just come out of its long war with Iraq and wanted us to import Lavan Blend and Iran Mix in as much quantity as possible. Lavan Blend and Iran Mix are Iranian crude oils. While Lavan Blend is a single blend, Iran Mix is a mixture of two crudes—Iran heavy and Iran light. Dr Ghanimi had a manager, Dr Babee, who was a Ph.D. from Pune University, and Bourjordi, a senior manager, who used to coordinate with international customers, to assist him. Both understood Hindi.

Knowing I hailed from Kashmir, conversations between us

became animated when Dr Ghanimi mentioned his plans to offer natural gas to India and Pakistan. 'Ashok, it will be a peace pipeline and you will be happy that the Kashmir problem will be resolved by better trade relations.' He proposed to discuss this during his next visit to Delhi. Iran had supported India in its stand on Kashmir for long, unlike most other countries.

About a decade later, in 2003, Usman Aminuddin, minister of petroleum under General Musharraf's regime, took the initiative to meet Ram Naik, the Indian petroleum minister on the sidelines of a Global Energy Conference held in Riyadh, Saudi Arabia. He suggested that India and Pakistan jointly negotiate with Iran for the Iran-Pakistan-India (IPI) gas pipeline because he, too, believed it would be a 'peace pipeline'. It was Usman Aminuddin who had signed detailed proposals with his Iranian counterpart, Bijan Namdar Zangeneh, in Islamabad on 22 February 2002 before formally commissioning a pre-feasibility study.

Ironically, the IPI gas pipeline project was initially supported by the US as well. A feasibility study was encouraged and Jaswant Singh from the BJP (Bhartiya Janata Party) and Mani Shankar Aiyar from the Indian National Congress (INC) even attended a review meeting as members of a Joint Working Group (JWG) in Singapore. I believe the IPI project will happen someday, as it is the most logical, practical and natural solution to our gas deficit, if only common sense prevails. Iran has the largest natural gas reserves in the world and people in India and Pakistan need access to an affordable and clean source of energy for economic progress and growth.

The interaction reminded me of Sheikh Abdullah's message that the way forward was to do away with the natural mistrust, fear and suspicions between India and Pakistan. On his way to hajj, he had said on 10 February 1963, while addressing the media at the Constitution Club, New Delhi, 'It is our firm belief that the salvation for the forty lakh people of Kashmir lies not in the contentions and confrontations between India and Pakistan but in friendship and understanding between them. As long as the conflict remains between them, Kashmiris will always suffer, for it is they who are stuck in this vortex.'[4]

Over fifty years later, mistrust, fear and suspicions have increased manifold. Kashmiriyat has not been understood by the outer world, and it is unfortunate that it is under attack in Kashmir as well. People with ethnic conflicts have to learn to work in a mutually beneficial way for a peaceful and prosperous society.

10

THE MISUNDERSTOOD MAHARAJA

As I look back at events after the accession of J&K with India in 1947, three key agreements merit attention—Instrument of Accession (1947), Simla Agreement (1972) and Indira-Sheikh Accord (1975). It is important to understand and recall the role of the three leaders (Maharaja Hari Singh, Sheikh Mohammad Abdullah and Indira Gandhi) and their expectations of deliverables.

Many remember Maharaja Hari Singh as the indecisive ruler who once preferred leisure (fishing and horse racing) over getting to business. He was also the man who was misunderstood by historical forces.

'My father Maharaja Hari Singh was a much "misunderstood man",[5] writes Dr Karan Singh in his foreword to the biography of his father by Professor Somnath Wakhlu. 'He was not enough of a diplomat like his great grandfather, Maharaja Gulab Singh, willing to modify his plans and schemes to suit the weather of destiny,' adds the biographer, Professor Wakhlu.[6]

THE REAL HARI SINGH

Who was the real Hari Singh? It is important to understand Hari Singh, as he was the central figure in the decision of the accession of J&K to India. He was a maharaja who spent most of his time in the paradise of his palaces and ruled the largest state in India. Its area was 222,236 square kilometres and its population, according to the census of 1941, was about forty lakhs (Muslims: 31,00,000; Hindus: 8,00,000; Sikhs: 65,000; Buddhists: 41,000 and others about 5,000).

For the purpose of administration, the state was divided into three provinces—Kashmir, Jammu and Ladakh & Gilgit Agency. While J&K was administered by two governors, a wazir wazarat, or a deputy commissioner, looked after Ladakh.

The Dogra rule did contribute positively to the development of J&K in many ways. Rerforms in administration, judiciary and revenue laws were promulgated as the Ranbir Penal Code, which is still followed in the state. Primary education was made free and compulsory. Child marriage was banned by law, though enforcement was feeble. People of all castes were allowed to enter temples, which is still an issue in mainland India. Connectivity was improved by building roads. A college and a hospital were opened in Srinagar as well as in Jammu. Municipalities were established. A hydropower station was started, perhaps the oldest in South Asia. However, the Dogras continued to be seen more as Hindu rulers by the Muslim majority in the state.

Maharaja Hari Singh, the last Dogra ruler, ascended the throne in 1925 and succeeded his uncle, Maharaja Pratap Singh, who had ruled the state for about forty years. During that time, the British had moved to Gilgit and Skardu to check the growing power of Russia. Pratap Singh was made to surrender power to a Council of Regency of the British with Anglo-Russian rivalry in mind.

Before his coronation, Hari Singh visited England for the first time in 1919. He was a young charming prince, 24 years of age, and the commander-in-chief of the state forces then. Captain C.W.A. Arthur, who had been deputed by the British government, accompanied the maharaja as his aid-de-camp, a personal assistant or secretary to a person of high rank. The British had taken a lot of interest in the education of Hari Singh after the death of his father in 1909.

On the night of 4 November 1919, the first anniversary of the signing of the armistice at the conclusion of the First World War (1914–1918), a victory ball was held in London. It was a great gathering of the high and mighty, of gallant men and beautiful ladies. The young Hari Singh was seated in a box in the front row. The next box had two charming ladies, Mrs Robinson and Mrs Bewan. Hari Singh and Mrs Robinson had a brief formal conversation. He made a stop in Paris on the way back home.

On one morning in December, Hari Singh and Mrs Robinson met clandestinely at Saint James, Paris. The door of the room had somehow been left open. Mrs Robinson's husband soon appeared on the scene, threatening divorce proceedings against her. ADC (Aid-de-camp) Captain Arthur seems to have prevailed upon Hari Singh to avoid being a co-respondent should Mrs Robinson receive a divorce petition from her husband, as that could derail his prospects of ascending the throne. They agreed to instead compensate her husband with two cheques of £150,000 each to avoid his going to court.[7]

While one of the cheques was encashed, a dispute seems to have arisen between Arthur and Mr Robinson. This matter reached the court, with Hari Singh remaining incognito as Mr A.

By the end of 1924, the case had leaked and became a sensational scandal. Mr A. became the central figure and the victim of a celebrated £300,000 (equivalent to $6 million today) blackmail case. His biographer, Professor Wakhlu, feels he was the victim of a conspiracy of the British, and that it was part of a strategy to control him to manage their Anglo-Russian plans when he ascended the throne.

In a paper entitled 'Blackmail' by Ronald H. Coarse, published by Chicago Law School in 1988, 'The Mr A. Case' is one of the case studies discussed at length. Apparently, Captain Arthur did tell Hari Singh that the scandal that would accompany such divorce proceedings would lead the India office to veto his accession to his uncle's throne. The Englishman who had entered the room was also not Mr Robinson but a Mr Newton, whose occupation was that of a 'confidence trickster, blackmailer, forger', etc. Whatever happened in that bedroom in Paris, Mr A. seems to have believed that Mr Newton was Mrs Robinson's husband. Perhaps this blackmailing case made Hari Singh nurture a dislike for the British and affected his subsequent relationship with them.

Hari Singh's personal life had many other setbacks. He married four times. The first three marriages included two wives from Saurashtra and one from Champa, now in Himachal Pradesh. His first wife died with a child in her womb, and the other two marriages did not bear him any children. To avoid being subject to the Doctrine of Lapse, whereby the British could take over the kingdom of the maharajas who did not bear any successor, he decided to marry a village girl, Tara Devi, from Kangra district, now in Himachal Pradesh. There was a good deal of tension and compatibility problems between the maharaja and the maharani. He was impulsive, given to sudden bursts of anger, pride and stubbornness, and did not know how to forgive and forget. While his wife was deeply religious, Hari Singh was a virtual agnostic. However, Swami Sant Dev, who was banished by Hari Singh when he ascended the throne, came back to live with them around 1944. Very soon, Hari Singh became his devout disciple. Swamiji had nursed a feudal ambition in Hari Singh of ruling an extended kingdom right till Lahore itself.

His son, Dr Karan Singh, in his books *Autobiography* and *The Heir Apparent*[8] recalls his father as affectionate enough, without being demonstrative. An excellent rider and a great polo player, he could not trust anyone for any length of time. He selected his prime ministers with great care, but no sooner had he appointed one than he would begin cultivating someone else as a sort of counterbalance. He was a lover of music as well as a good shooter. However, as is common to the feudal order, he was a bad loser, whether in shooting, fishing or riding.

MISTRUST OF THE BRITISH

Hari Singh genuinely distrusted the British and had the courage to take many first steps in India, ahead of his time. He allowed people of lower castes, Harijans, to enter temples, and took many social welfare measures.

On 12 November 1930 Hari Singh went to represent Indian princes at the first round table conference (RTC) between the British, the Indian state representatives and the British Indian representatives. He was accompanied by Col Kailash Nath Haksar. The idea of an All India Federation was moved to the centre of the discussion by Tej Bahadur Sapru at this conference. All the members of the group attending the conference supported his concept. However, the princely states agreed to the proposed federation, provided their internal sovereignty was guaranteed.

Addressing the first RTC meeting, which was the opening ceremony, hence very important to set the direction of the meeting, Maharaja Hari Singh stated in a patriotic manner that Indians stood firmly for a position of honour and equality in the British Commonwealth of Nations, with a willingness to extend full cooperation towards all sections of opinion and stakeholders in the conference.

When Kabali tribal raiders from Pakistan invaded Kashmir in October 1947, my father had just begun his career in Baramulla at the age of 20 after the untimely death of my paternal grandfather. Like all others, he had to flee to Srinagar to save his life. Whatever belongings he had were left behind. He recalled the role played by Sherwani, a Kashmiri youth and National Conference member, at the cost of his life while regretting the indecisiveness of Maharaja Hari Singh to decide either way on accession. Sherwani was about 19 years old when the Kabali raiders reached Baramulla. Thousands of raiders were within thirty miles of Srinagar. The leader of the tribals asked Sherwani for directions to reach Srinagar. He misguided them by giving them wrong directions, and they lost four precious days, in which time the Indian Army reached Srinagar. When Sherwani was captured by raiders and asked to direct them to the airport, he refused to comply and was put on a wooden cross, nailed and fired upon. He was one of the greatest saviours who prevented Kashmir from falling into the hands of Pakistan in 1947. I recall reading *Death of a Hero* by well-known author Mulk Raj Anand, giving an account of Sherwani's story.

My father also recalled that Maqbool was a dedicated activist of the National Conference. When Mohammad Ali Jinnah visited Kashmir and spoke of his two-nation theory, Maqbool forced him to stop his speech. He was clearly an ardent supporter of

Sheikh Abdullah's policy of aligning with the Indian state on secular values.

After his opening address as the pro-chancellor on behalf of the princes of India, the British looked at Hari Singh with suspicion. He was the one willing to bat straight. The British had strengthened their hold on the state, and he wanted to curtail their domination.

Maharaja Hari Singh did not trust the British, and they, too, had no love for him. When Lord Mountbatten visited Kashmir as the viceroy to persuade him to make up his mind before 15 August 1947, Hari Singh sent him to Thricker, near Pahalgam in Kashmir, on a fishing trip. He was supposed to have brought an assurance from Indian leaders that they would not take any objection to whatever decision the maharaja would take, including accession to Pakistan. The maharaja did not trust the viceroy. The latter made good use of his time at Thricker for fishing.

The maharaja did not avail of the opportunity to have a meaningful dialogue on three possible options—independence, accession to Pakistan or accession to India—and gain by insight and advice of the viceroy. When the viceroy returned from his fishing trip and fixed a meeting with the maharaja before his departure, Hari Singh cancelled it on the pretext of a severe colic attack. The maharaja also harboured similar dislike for people like Sheikh Abdullah, Jinnah and, above all, Nehru.

Even when uncertainty and tension were mounting, Maharaja Hari Singh devoted his love for horse racing in Poona. With stake winnings of ₹52,500, the maharaja topped the list of winning owners for Poona Racing Season, which closed on 5 October 1947.

WEIGHING THE SCALES OF ACCESSION

One of the possible factors that could have weighed on his mind against accession to India was the treatment of Muslims in a Hindu majority country. The maharaja understandably would have had apprehensions about the survival of a Muslim-majority state in a Hindu-majority India, notwithstanding the fact that there would have been more Muslims in post-Partition India than in Pakistan.

Maharaja Hari Singh had been advised a number of times by Mahatma Gandhi and Sardar Patel to join either dominion. Mahatma Gandhi in his post-prayer speech on 27 July 1947 drew the attention of the people to the conference of rulers of the princely states called by the viceroy. Since the British could not compel them to join one or the other dominion, the viceroy added that it would be wise for the princes to make their choice by paying due regard to their geographical position and ethno-religious composition of the state.[9]

Operationally and logistically, pre-Independent J&K had no link with the Indian Union of the post-Partition era. It was only on 28 July 1947 that the J&K government sanctioned a scheme for metalling the Kathua road. This decision could have been a preparatory step in his plan of accession to India, if any. By 25 September, the Kashmir government ordered the construction of a boat bridge over the river Ravi near Pathankot, thus connecting J&K to the Indian Union. Parallely, the work on the construction of a new road from Jammu city to Kathua on the Jammu state border touching Gurudaspur district in east Punjab ensued. Christopher Beaumont, private secretary to British lawyer Cyril Radcliffe who was appointed the task of drawing the boundaries of the new nations of Pakistan and India, stated after Radcliffe's death that no change was made in the northern Gurdaspur line and it was always proposed to be given to India. Had these developments not taken place, operationally there would have been little favouring accession of the state to India.[10]

I never got to see Maharaja Hari Singh but I did get to hear Sheikh Abdullah on many occasions from 1974 to 1977 in person, and even shake hands with him once in 1977, when I received a merit certificate from him during his visit to our engineering college.

While it is true that India did not accept the two-nation theory of Partition based on religion and emerged as a secular country, it is also noteworthy to recall that Jinnah had not imagined a Pakistan that has evolved post the Zia-ul-Haq era. Taking a call on the accession of his state to Pakistan based on the majority Muslim population or acceding to India based on perceived secular democratic values or opting to remain independent, with good relations with both countries—it couldn't have been an easy choice for any ruler.

There was an influential section of political leadership which was reconciled to the possibility of Maharaja Hari Singh acceding to Pakistan. If the rationale for the accession of Junagarh or Hyderabad to India was justified on the grounds that these were Hindu-majority princely states ruled by Muslim rulers, it would be morally incorrect to support accession of a Muslim-majority state to India which was ruled by a Hindu monarch. If India-held people were sovereign in case of Junagarh and Hyderabad, the same would have applied to Kashmir as well. But the sheer presence and leadership of Sheikh Abdullah tilted the scales in favour of secular India. Hari Singh will remain a 'misunderstood maharaja', whose hands were forced by aggression from Pakistan.

11

SHEIKH ABDULLAH'S KASHMIR SAGA

As I heard Sheikh Abdullah's speeches from 1974 to 1977, little did I realize that each of his earlier statements would contribute, bit by bit, to the shaping of the political destiny of Kashmir, although not in the manner dreamt by him.

From 1947, plebiscite, self-determination, independence and Indo-Pak amity dominated the discourse in Kashmir. And, if there was one person who had devoted most of his life to these themes, especially from 1947 to 1975, it was Sheikh Mohammad Abdullah. Some of his statements made prior to 1974 led to the Sheikh-Indira Accord of 1975, which paved the way to his becoming the chief minister of J&K in 1975. It was generally concluded after his accord that demands for plebiscite, self-determination and independence were closed chapters for Kashmir.

As the head of the interim government of J&K, Sheikh Abdullah addressed a gathering of Americans at a luncheon of the India League of America hosted in his honour on 26 January 1948.[11]

Sheikh Abdullah stressed that were it not for the assistance received from the Government of India, Kashmir would have either had to surrender to Pakistan or perish. He denounced the two-nation theory for bringing about devastation in the Valley.

While he had unflinching faith in Kashmir's resistance to enslavement by Pakistan, he also believed that a solution to this main irritant could open the floodgate of friendship between the two countries.

Regrettably, Maharaja Hari Singh had remained undecided for long to create conditions for Pakistan to create pressure. His letter seeking accession to India was unconditional, and India's response was constitutionally correct and appropriate. Lord Mountbatten had noted with satisfaction that the maharaja had decided to invite Sheikh Abdullah to form the interim government. Mountbatten had also agreed to resolve the question of accession in the light of the wishes of the people of the state by stating that 'as soon as law and order have been restored in J&K and her soil cleared of the invader, the question of the state's accession should be settled by a reference to the people'.

1952 AGREEMENT

On 1 May 1951, Yuvraj Karan Singh made a proclamation convening the Constituent Assembly. Of the seventy-five seats, nominees of the National Conference were elected unopposed on most occasions. Addressing the Assembly on 31 October 1951, Sheikh Abdullah said, 'There are three issues before the Kashmir constituent assembly, namely, accession to India, accession to Pakistan and remaining independent. I have now put the pros and cons of the three alternatives before you. It should not be difficult for men of discrimination and patriotism gathered in the assembly to weigh all these with scales of our national good and pronounce where the true well-being of the country lies in the future.' He ruled out the last two options and expressed his own preference for accession to India.

After the constituent assembly arrived at its main conclusion, Sheikh Abdullah met Pandit Nehru and arrived at the Delhi Agreement, 1952. The Government of India agreed that while the residual powers of legislation vested in the Centre in respect of all states, in the case of J&K they were vested in the state itself. Persons domiciled in J&K shall be regarded as citizens of India, but the state legislature was empowered to make laws for conferring special rights and privileges on the state's subjects. The Sadar-i-Riyasat, equivalent to the governor of other states, was to be elected by the state legislature itself instead of being nominated by the Union government and the president of India.

The understanding formed the basis for the incorporation of Article 370 in the Indian Constitution under 'Temporary provisions with respect to the state of J&K.'

Meanwhile, on 21 October 1951, Dr Shyama Prasad Mukherjee founded Bharatiya Jana Sangh and became its first president. He had participated in the cabinet meeting that decided to approach the UN on the issue of aggression by Pakistan in J&K post its accession to India. However, he became the voice of the people who were upset with provisions made under Article 370. He raised the slogan, 'Ek desh mein do vidhan, do nishan, do pradhan—nahi chalenge' meaning 'One constitution, one flag and one president' for full integration with India, and he supported the Praja Parishad Party of J&K. Dr Mukherjee was detained in Srinagar for more than a month and died in Kashmir during detention under mysterious circumstances on 23 June 1953.[12]

Well after the Constitution of India with Article 370 came into force, the continued approach of the Government of India that Kashmir was an 'open' issue created uncertainty in the state. The government led by Sheikh Abdullah took a lead from this approach of Delhi and placed the matter before the working committee of the National Conference, which met in May 1953. It appointed an eight-member committee to explore avenues of a settlement and kept Nehru informed of the deliberations. The committee arrived at the following proposals in its final session, held on 9 June 1953, as possible alternatives to an honourable and peaceful solution of the Kashmir dispute between India and Pakistan.

(a) Overall plebiscite
(b) Independence of the whole state
(c) Independence of the whole state with joint control by India and Pakistan of foreign affairs
(d) Dixon plan with independence for the plebiscite area

As per the Dixon plan, while India would have retained Jammu and Ladakh, and Pakistan would have retained Gilgit-Baltistan, Kashmir and PoK (Pakistan-occupied Kashmir) would be put to plebiscite.[13]

Nehru had meetings with Mohammad Ali Bogra, prime minister of Pakistan from 25 July to 27 July 1953 to decide the future of the state. However, immediately thereafter, Sheikh Abdullah was arrested, along with some of his colleagues, on the night of 8 August 1953 on charges of conspiring with the US. The two prime ministers again met in Delhi between 17 August and 20 August 1953 and reiterated their resolve to settle the dispute in accordance with the wishes of the people.

A year and a half later, Govind Ballabh Pant, the Union Home Minister, confirmed Nehru's altered stance in his speech in Srinagar on 7 July 1955: 'Kashmir's accession was a reality

SHEIKH ABDULLAH'S KASHMIR SAGA ◆ 105

which could not be changed because the people, through the representatives in the Constituent Assembly, had decided to remain with India.'

Thus, Pant ruled out plebiscite in Kashmir because he did not see any prospect of Pakistan agreeing to honourable conditions on the issue. A month later, Bakshi Ghulam Mohammad, who had in the meeting of the eight-member committee advocated the adoption of the Dixon Plan declared in Srinagar on 24 August 1955 that no plebiscite would be held in the state 'till eternity'.

The Kashmir constituent assembly adopted a constitution on 17 November 1956, which was to come into force from 26 January 1957. The people of Azad Kashmir had not voted for the constituent assembly. Twenty-five seats were left vacant 'until the area of the state under occupation of Pakistan ceases to be so occupied and the people residing in that area elect their representative'.

As events unfolded from 1948 to 1953, leading to Sheikh Abdullah's dismissal and arrest in 1953, he was saddled with the stupendous task of finding a lasting solution in the fast-changing political environment in South Asia. The complexity of the situation is not hard to surmise. After spending over ten years under arrest, his statement on 9 May 1964 after release focussed on emphasizing that 'Kashmir's accession to India was neither final nor irrevocable'.[14]

Two days later, on 11 May, Sheikh Abdullah told *The Times of India* in Mumbai that he was striving to bring India and Pakistan together for the solution of the Kashmir problem, along with 'other points of friction'. He pleaded for an objective review of the Kashmir problem. 'I am setting aside the question of accession of Kashmir to India for the time being. We may say the accession is final, but we cannot deny the existence of the problem. By merely saying that there is no question of accession, the issue does not get resolved,' he stated.

Most opinion makers and legal experts in India and abroad have continued to be of the view that the accession of J&K to India is valid, final and irrevocable. Further, the maharaja of J&K, Hari Singh, an absolute monarch, was within his rights to either accede to India or to Pakistan or to retain his independent status as a separate state, if he so decided. I discussed this issue with Justice Chittatosh Mookerjee, former chief justice of the Calcutta and Bombay high courts. He said that a solution had to be arrived at—political, economic and constitutional—for the Kashmir problem but did not foresee any change in the structure of Article 370. There was no scope of trading on the question of the integration of Kashmir into India and recognizing the ceasefire line as the line of demarcation into two parts. The problem he saw looming large was the problem of radicalization, and he upheld the right of the Kashmiri Pandits to return to the Valley. Pandits have a deep culture, a tradition and a religion of their own, and their dispersal hurt Kashmiri traditions that had been preserved for thousands of years, he added.

As Pakistan lost its eastern province in 1971, leading to the creation of Bangladesh, the contours of a future solution for Kashmir changed as well. India and Pakistan agreed to a discussion for a final negotiated solution on Kashmir and resolved to do so through bilateral discussions without recourse to force, overtly or covertly, as per the Simla Agreement of 1972.

On 10 August 1972, it became public that Indira Gandhi had expressed a desire to Sheikh Abdullah 'to open a new chapter in Indo-Kashmir relations'. Addressing a public meeting at 'Mujahid Manzil' to observe what has been called the Black Day to protest against Sheikh Abdullah's dismissal from office on 9 August 1953,

Abdullah said the wishes of the Kashmiri people would be kept in mind in any settlement on the question. The prime minister's 'offer' to open a new chapter after a lapse of nineteen years now appeared to be the result of the 'awakening of conscience' of the Indian leadership, he added.

Sheikh Abdullah realized that Pakistan was weakened further post the 1971 war with India that led to the liberation of Bangladesh. His accord with Indira Gandhi that made him chief minister had focussed on the retention of Article 370 to assure the majority community in the state that there was no danger while merging with India.

However, the nomenclature of the governor and the chief minister was remitted to the principals, as no agreement could be resolved between Afzal Beg, lawyer and politician, acting on behalf of Sheikh Abdullah, and G. Parthasarathy, diplomat, acting on behalf of the government headed by Indira Gandhi. The Government of India can re-visit this issue with the elected legislature of J&K and agree on nomenclature.

Addressing a press conference in Jammu on 3 March 1975,[15] Sheikh Abdullah clarified that his objective was to clear the old atmosphere of mistrust and further the 'accession of minds' between the people of J&K and the rest of the country.

Sheikh Abdullah was right. Gopalaswami Ayyangar had managed to persuade Sardar Patel and Maulana Azad to convince the Congress party to approve his formulation of proposals before they were put before the Congress party at the constituent assembly. It was Sardar Patel who pointed out the delicate international position of the state and the issue of its relationship with India. Nehru was abroad when the Congress approved proposals of Ayyangar that became the bedrock of Article 370.

According to Sheikh Abdullah, no government in J&K would be able to function unless it assured both the majority and the minority that their fears of being overwhelmed by each other were groundless. With such a clear objective in mind, Sheikh Abdullah assumed power in January 1975 after his accord with Indira Gandhi. It had seemingly helped to put an end to over two decades of misunderstandings.

Syed Mir Qasim, who had stepped down as chief minister in an act of self-abnegation as per terms of the accord could claim some credit for the Kashmir accord. Sheikh Abdullah had no animosity towards Syed Mir Qasim or the Congress after assuming power in 1975. He desired a merger of the state Congress party with the National Conference party. He felt that the presence of a single party of like-minded people would be more conducive to development of the state. Regrettably, based on feedback and discussions with state Congress leaders, Indira Gandhi ruled out such a merger. Sheikh Abdullah wanted the National Conference to be the sole party to function in the state for five years. If it failed to deliver the goods, it could be rejected. He earnestly believed that by virtue of its historic role, it had a better claim. One wonders how events would have taken shape had Indira Gandhi agreed to his suggestion. India has seen regional parties like the DMK (Dravida Munnetra Kazhagam) or the AIADMK (All India Anna Dravida Munnetra Kazhagam) dominate politics in states like Tamil Nadu, with national parties playing a side role. In a sensitive state like Kashmir, it could have helped satisfy the local identity of the J&K polity. But Indira Gandhi followed a different strategy than her father, Jawaharlal Nehru. He never allowed the Congress to exist in J&K. He only worked through a wing of the National Conference. Perhaps he understood Kashmiri sentiments much better and saw no harm in a local party governing Kashmir as long as it was wedded to secular and liberal values of the Indian Constitution.

There is little dispute that elections from 1952 to 1977 were manipulated, rigged and unfair. My dear friend, Dr Manzoor Qazi, a highly respected orthopaedic surgeon today, was a student of the Government Medical College in Srinagar and an activist. He was president of the youth wing set up by Pir Giasuddin, a former Industries minister, to fight election to the state assembly in 1972 when Mir Qasim was the chief minister. Three hundred and thirty seven candidates contested the elections for sixty-nine assembly seats for which polling was held in March. Of these, 190 were in the Valley and the rest in the Jammu region. It was an election when a maximum number of independent candidates, 119 of the 190, contested for thirty-nine seats in the Valley. It was also the first election when three women candidates contested the assembly polls in the Valley.[16]

Manzoor and his friends cast thousands of proxy votes in ballot boxes in favour of their leader. In the evening, when the election results were announced, they were surprised to hear that the votes polled by their leader were less than what they had put in the boxes themselves at various booths, not including the votes cast in his favour by the general public.

Agitated, all polling staff led by Manzoor went to the residence of Syed Mir Qasim to challenge the result. He calmed them down and told them that he could do little as the name of their leader and his ex-colleague was not in the list of candidates to be declared elected as received from Delhi!

I also recall that in the elections held in 1972, my paternal grandmother asked me to accompany her to the polling booth. Elections were being held to elect members to the legislative assembly. The polling booth was in DAV school in Jawahar Nagar, very close to our residence. The polling agent told me that since I was not a registered voter, I could not accompany her inside the booth. While he was talking to me, two election agents came from inside and asked, 'Dadi, why have you come to the booth?'

She replied, 'I have come to cast my vote, what else?'

They retorted, 'We know who you will cast your vote for. You support the Congress. We have voted on your behalf for the Congress'. Being in my late teens, I was infuriated by the lack of transparency and retorted sharply, telling them that they were engaging in illegal practices. One of the election agents came out and told me, 'Go away, you batta, we know you are dhai Congress. When you become a voter, we know who you will vote for.'

In those years, Kashmiri Pandits were popularly perceived as staunch supporters of the Congress. Hence, dhai Congress meant that one person was equal to two and a half Congress supporters. Such inferences were natural, as this miniscule community had given four elected presidents to the Congress, who steered its destiny for a long period, namely, Bishan Narayan Dar (1911), Motilal Kaul Nehru (1919 and 1928), Jawaharlal Nehru (1929 and 1930, 1936–1937 and 1951–1954) and Indira Gandhi (1959 and 1979–1984). Regrettably, the Congress did little to prevent the exodus of the Kashmiri Pandits in 1990, and the community has paid a heavy price for being related to a select few who rose to positions of power and authority by dint of their hard work, honesty and merit. The average Kashmiri Pandit in the Valley was either a teacher, a lecturer or a clerk in government offices, banks or in the private sector. With a population of a few lakhs, the miniscule minority is irrelevant as a vote bank, except for being used for electoral rhetoric to serve political agendas of various parties.

Plebiscite, self-determination, independence—all were evaluated by Sheikh Abdullah before entering the 1975 Indira–Sheikh accord. If only all parties had been sincere enough to implement the understanding in letter and spirit, Kashmir could have avoided the loss of a generation, bloodshed and the exodus of a population.

LESSONS FROM SHEIKH ABDULLAH

One of the less-frequently discussed issues is the review of the post-1953 laws in J&K by Sheikh Abdullah when he resumed power after the accord in 1975. The cabinet had appointed two committees under the chairmanship of Mirza Mohammad Afzal Beg, deputy chief minister under Sheikh Abdullah. Devi Das Thakur, law minister, was included in both the committees. One of the two committees was asked to conduct a critical examination of the provisions of the Constitution of India and the laws extended to the state after 1953. The other committee was asked to examine preventive detention laws in force in the state, the life of which had been extended periodically, and the last extension had also expired.

The committee for the review of the post-1953 laws met twice or thrice but there was a sharp division amongst the members on the desirability of the review or revocation of the laws that the Constitution extended to the state after 1953. This had caused a stalemate. The committee had continued to exist even after 1979 and Afzal Beg resigned from the cabinet, with D.D. Thakur as its chairman. A few meetings held under his chairmanship proved inconclusive. Sometime in 1980, chief minister Sheikh

Abdullah decided that the committee should present a report without further delay. Ghulam Mohammad Shah and Ghulam Nabi Kochak complained to the chief minister that the meeting could not be held because of the non-availability of Devi Dass Thakur on account of his other engagements. It was at this stage that Devi Dass Thakur proposed to the chief minister that he be allowed to submit his report, and that Shah and Kochak submit their report separately. Both Kochak and Shah submitted their report within a week of Thakur's submission of his. The reports were at variance with each other.[17]

Thakur opposed any further deliberation on the question in view of what had been committed by the accord on behalf of Sheikh Abdullah and Mohammad Afzal Beg. Paragraphs 14 and 15 of the report of Thakur gave an interesting rationale, emphasizing on the need for a common basis to evolve, as any unilateral action would result in a reversal of constitutional developments since 1953. Such an action would also jeopardize the Accord of 1975.[18] This appeared to have been appreciated by Sheikh Abdullah, because of which the question of review was not raised in the cabinet thereafter, till his demise in 1982.

It is surprising that even after almost four decades of the Thakur report, the government has not made public the comments on file on the review of the post-1953 laws. When I met Radha Kumar, one of the three interlocutors appointed by the United Progressive Alliance (UPA-1), she told me that they had no access to any government files!

Did Sheikh Abdullah write words like 'not relevant now' or 'no looking back' on the file for review of the post-1953 laws and indeed appreciate the rationale given by Thakur? That can only be known if the files are made public. The fact that not much was done by Sheikh Abdullah to review the post-1953 laws between 1975 and 1982 could also perhaps be due to his realization that the Constitution was indeed fair to its citizens and did not discriminate between people based on region, gender, race and religion. After all, Sheikh Abdullah, along with his three colleagues, were members of the constituent assembly that drafted the Indian Constitution.

I believe there is a lesson from Sheikh's Kashmir saga. Can his Accord of 1975 become the real Magna Carta for preservation of autonomy of the state if the Government of India were to announce a time-bound commitment to implement the same in letter and spirit? Also, what if Article 370 is made a special permanent feature of the Indian Constitution?

12

SIMLA ACCORD—THE REAL STORY

When Nehru signed an agreement to demarcate the border on the basis of a ceasefire line with Pakistan PM Mohammad Ali Bogra, nobody could have guessed his daughter, too, would follow in his footsteps over fifteen years later, when she would sign the Simla Accord on 2 July 1972 with Zulfikar Ali Bhutto in Simla. Whether there was a secret understanding to this effect in Simla in addition to the accord signed has remained a mystery, though some believe that the document incorporating the discussion between the two leaders is in possession of the Government of India.

For Kashmiris, the Simla negotiation should have settled the dispute once and for all. The Indian delegation accompanying Indira Gandhi included knowledgeable and high-ranking members of the biradari. D.P. Dhar, key advisor to Indira Gandhi, was the Indian emissary who prepared the agenda for talks with his counterpart from Pakistan—Aziz Ahmed, at Murree, Pakistan, on 26 April 1971.

If there was anyone who knew the deep dynamics of internal politics in J&K, it was Dhar, since he was a close associate of

Sheikh Abdullah, Bakshi Ghulam Mohammad and G.M. Sadiq. He was renowned for his intellect. He had played a key role in the negotiation of the Indo-Soviet Treaty of Peace, Friendship and Cooperation, which had helped in the liberation of East Pakistan.

T.N. Kaul, the Indian foreign secretary, P.N. Dhar, the principal secretary, and P.N. Haksar, former diplomat, were other Kashmiris helping Indira Gandhi in Simla.

Both delegations had different immediate and long-term objectives. Pakistan wanted the return of its 5,000-square-mile territories under Indian occupation, the return of nearly 92,000–97,000 POWs and to avoid a settlement of Kashmir. On the other hand, India wanted to leverage her position post-war to secure a final settlement on Kashmir.

SIMLA CONFERENCE—A 'BREAKTHROUGH'

The Simla Agreement was drafted on 28 June 1972. After the exchange of formal greetings, Indira Gandhi and Zulfikar Bhutto met separately in a restricted session with key aides. They nominated D.P. Dhar and Aziz Ahmed as leaders for the delegation to start negotiations.

The next four days were full of intense negotiations and possible compromise. After the treaty presented by India was rejected by Pakistan, D.P. Dhar suffered a heart attack and was not available for further negotiation. This was a great loss to India because he had diplomatic experience and a deep knowledge of Kashmir politics. To break the deadlock, Indira Gandhi and Bhutto met twice, followed by the resumption of talks between the delegations.

Even after the 1 July meeting between Indira Gandhi and Bhutto, there was no progress. The talks were resumed by P.N.

Haksar and Aziz Ahmed. Haksar presented a revised draft, and India offered withdrawal of troops from positions held to international border reciprocally. The Line of Control (LoC) was to be respected by both sides. However, there was no reference to either prisoners of war (POWs) or ceasefire lines. In the evening, Indira Gandhi and Bhutto met again along with their principal aides. But success to strike an agreement eluded them.

Both delegations worked to make progress on 2 July without a day of rest. Pakistan returned India's draft with changes that were unacceptable to India.

At noon Haksar and Kaul called on Bhutto with India's final draft and conveyed the message from the prime minister that it was reasonable, indicating that it was the farthest India could go.

Kaul asked Bhutto, 'Mr President, when you were the foreign minister, you said at the Tashkent Conference (1966) that Kashmir was the root cause of all Indo-Pak differences. Today you are the president and have the opportunity of reaching a peaceful and final settlement of this question. Will you do it?'[19]

Bhutto replied, 'You are correct, Mr Kaul. I did say this in Tashkent. But today I represent a defeated country. Give me a few weeks more and as soon as I go back, I shall prepare the ground for it.'[20]

The officials met at 3.30 p.m. on 2 July but could make no progress. Kaul, addressing a press conference, declared that talks had broken down, and left for Chandigarh. Bhutto decided to pay a farewell visit to the prime minister and use the protocol visit to try one last time with Indira Gandhi.

Dhar, principal secretary to Indira Gandhi, was perhaps the closest person within hearing distance of whatever Bhutto discussed with her. He recalled in a newspaper article that Indira Gandhi elaborated the merits of the Indian proposal on Kashmir and sold it as the only feasible solution.[21] An important feature of the proposal was that neither side was gaining or losing territory on account of the war. It also did not involve any transfer with respect to population. Kashmir as an ethnic side was left undivided on the Indian side. The LoC was, therefore, an ethnic and linguistic frontier.

In fact, in 1947, it was also an ideological frontier, being the limit of political influence of Sheikh Adbullah and his National Conference (NC) party, notwithstanding his claim to be the undisputed leader of undivided J&K. True, there were some anomalies in this otherwise neatly etched picture but, these, Indira Gandhi pointed out, could be removed by mutual consent.

Dhar recalled that Bhutto responded with feeling and apparent sincerity. After a long and agonizing reflection, Bhutto said he too had concluded that the Indian proposal was the only feasible one. He would, however, work towards its implementation in practice and over time. Indira Gandhi herself was worried that a formal withdrawal of the Indian claim on PoK could create political trouble for her. She agreed that the solution should not be recorded in the agreement for reasons advanced by Bhutto, but it should be gradually implemented, as suggested by Bhutto. It was also agreed that the understanding would not be a written one. The insertion of a secret clause in the agreement was considered inconsistent with the desire to build a structure of durable peace. They decided to word the agreement in such a way that it could facilitate the implementation of the understanding. This is what resulted in the last-minute negotiations carried out during the return banquet of the president of Pakistan on the eve of his departure.

While the media hailed the agreement as a breakthrough, a reporter for *The Times* in London, Peter Hazelhurst, wrote on 4

July 1972 that it was also a concession to Indira Gandhi, who had advocated bilateralism as a means of settling Kashmir and other disputes with Pakistan.

The truth, according to Dhar, was that Bhutto had agreed not only to change the ceasefire line to the LoC, but had also agreed that the line could be gradually endowed with the 'characteristics of an international border' (Bhutto's words).[22] The idea was to allow traffic at specific points on the LoC and to slowly allow customs and immigration. Bhutto's political party would have set up its branches and later the area would have been taken over by the administration. India would protest, just for the sake of protest.[23] Well, many would have forgotten that this was what happened subsequently when PoK and Gilgit-Baltistan became a province of Pakistan.

Bhutto and Mrs Gandhi thought that with the gradual use of the LoC as a de-facto frontier, public opinion would be reconciled to its permanence. Meanwhile, the opening of trade and commerce and co-operation would result in easing tensions between the two countries.

Indira Gandhi, after recounting their points of agreement, finally asked Bhutto, 'Is this the understanding on which we will proceed?'

He replied, 'Absolutely, *aap mujh par bharosa keejiye* [please trust me].'[24]

One of Bhutto's aides, who was close to the Americans, fully briefed James P. Sterba, the *New York Times* correspondent, on the Bhutto-Gandhi understanding. In his news analysis, which appeared within hours of the signing of the agreement, Sterba wrote, 'President Bhutto, Pakistan's first civilian leader in fourteen years, came to Simla ready to compromise.'

The *New York Times* on 3 July reported that according to

sources close to Bhutto, he was willing to forsake the India-held two-thirds of Kashmir that contained four-fifths of the population and the prized Valley, called Vale, and agree that a ceasefire line—to be negotiated—would gradually became the border between the two countries. The keyword was 'gradually'. President Bhutto wanted a softening of the ceasefire line—with trade and travel across it—and a secret agreement with Indira Gandhi that a formally recognized border would emerge after a year, during which he would condition his people to it without riots and an overthrow of his government.

A MISSED OPPURTUNITY

It was indeed a unique gesture, as India could have refused to return over 5,000 square miles and 92,000 POWs unless Pakistan agreed to a final, peaceful settlement of Kashmir. Perhaps Dhar would have prevailed upon Indira Gandhi to follow this line had he not suffered an untimely heart attack. But Mrs Gandhi was magnanimous in her victory and did not want Bhutto to go 'empty-handed' as he pleaded. She hoped that this gesture would be appreciated by Pakistan.

Bhutto's successors have carried an open interference in the Indian side of the Line of Control in blatant violation of the Simla Agreement, but India still hopes that Pakistan will see the wisdom of settling the issue peacefully and bilaterally under the Simla Agreement.

When Bhutto came to Simla, he knew well that Sheikh Abdullah's political differences with the Government of India were being sorted out.[25] From his own sources and from reports in the Indian press, he was aware of the possibility of Sheikh Abdullah joining mainstream politics. In fact, G. Parthasarathy, who was the son of N. Gopalaswami Ayyangar, a minister in Nehru's cabinet, had already begun a round of talks with Sheikh Abdullah before the Simla Summit. Three weeks after signing the Simla Agreement, the ban on the entry of Sheikh Abdullah to Kashmir was removed. Sheikh Abdullah, while addressing his audience in Srinagar, told them on entry to Srinagar how correct Kashmir was in rejecting a union with theocratic Pakistan. Sheikh Abdullah's withdrawal of his demand for a plebiscite was expected to help Bhutto in facing the criticism of people at home. Mirza Afzal Beg, who led the plebiscite front, also declared it as irrelevant in the changed circumstances.

Regrettably, we have not been able to build upon the understandings: neither of the Sheikh accord, nor of the Simla Agreement. Kashmiris at the helm had an opportunity in Simla that does not recur often in history. Destiny, our taqdeer! But the accord avoided a major war between India and Pakistan and has remained an umbrella agreement and a benchmark for future dialogue.

ENDNOTES

1   Verghese Kothiara, *Crafting Peace in Kashmir: Through a Realist Lens*, Sage Publications, 2004.

2   Sumit Ganguly, *The Crisis in Kashmir: Portents of War, Hopes of Peace*. Woodrow Wilson Center Press and Cambridge University Press, USA, 1998.

3   'Kashmir Teen Killed during Anti-Israel Rally', *Aj Jazeera*, 20 July 2014.

4   Sheikh Mohammad Abdullah, *The Blazing Chinar*, Srinagar: Gulshan Books, 2013.

5   Somnath Wakhlu, *The Rich Heritage of Jammu and Kashmir: Studies*

in Art, Architecture, History and Culture of the Region. New Delhi: Gyan Publishing House, 1998.

6   Ibid.

7   Ronald H. Coase, 'Blackmail', Occasional Papers, University of Chicago Law School, 1988.

8   Somnath Wakhlu, *Hari Singh: The Maharaja, The Man, The Times,* National Publishing House, 2006.

9   'Respect People's Paramountcy: Join One or Other Dominion— Mahatma Gandhi's Plea to Princes', *The Times of India,* 28 July 1947.

10   Prem Shankar Jha, *Kashmir 1947: Rival Versions of History,* India: Oxford Univerity Press, 1996.

11   'Kashmir will Not Tolerate Enslavement by Pakistan: Sheikh Abdullah Explains Stand on Accession Issue', *The Times of India,* 28 January 1948.

12   Devesh Khandelwal (ed.), *Pledge for an Integrated India,* Prabhat Parkashan, 2015.

13   A.G. Noorani, 'The Dixon Plan', *Frontline,* Volume 19, Issue 21, 12–25 October, 2002.

14   'Indo-Pak Amity: Abdullah', *The Times of India,* Bombay, 10 May 1964.

15   'Accord Only First Step: Sheikh', *The Times of India,* 4 March 1975.

16   'Independents Dominate in Kashmir', *The Times of India,* 13 February 1972

17   D.D. Thakur, *My Life and Years in Kashmir Politics,* Konark Publishers, p 289, 2005.

18   D.D. Thakur, *My Life and Years in Kashmir Politics,* Konark Publishers, pp 288–290, 2005.

19   T.N. Kaul, 'What is at Stake in Kashmir?', *Koshur Samachar,* Oct–Nov 1992.

20.   T.N. Kaul, 'What is at Stake in Kashmir?', *Koshur Samachar,* p 6, Oct–Nov 1992.

21 P.N. Dhar, 'Kashmir: The Simla Solution', *The Times of India*, 4 April 1995.

22 Ibid.

23 Ibid.

24 Ibid.

25 Addendum: Dhar on Kashmir, *The Times of India*, 5 April 1995.

PART-III

MY DESTINY

13

REBELLIOUS DECADE

The Simla Accord helped Sheikh Abdullah accept the geopolitical reality and seek a Pareto Optimal solution by signing the accord in 1975. The subsequent rebellion in the 1990s and the exodus of the Kashmiri Hindus (1990) altered the narrative of Kashmir. Efforts via backchannelling to resolve the dispute amongst all parties is yet to bear fruit. We have to look at issues dispassionately to decide a forward path to help shape our destiny.

EARLY MILITANCY

Although militancy in Kashmir is said to have commenced in 1989, I remember terrorist activity from the 1970s. From the mid-1960s to the 1970s, many underground cells such as Al-Fatah, Al-Baro and Al-Kashmir, allegedly financed by Pakistan, were unearthed by the J&K police. However, these terrorist outfits did not get any support from the local population. In 1986, when the Congress party withdrew support from chief minister G.M. Shah, the Valley began to experience widespread resentment against New Delhi. Shah's tenure was marked by anarchy and maladministration. He also raised the '*Islam khatre mein hain*' (Islam is in danger) slogan, which fuelled communal tensions that later exploded into a major upheaval. Consequently, the goodwill that was generated after the Simla Accord was lost.

In November 1986, Dr Farooq Abdullah was reinstated as the chief minister of Kashmir, heading a coalition government of the National Conference and the Congress. However, after the heavy rigging of the elections in 1987 under the auspices of the National Conference, conditions conducive to supporting militancy were again generated in the Valley. Therefore, we cannot deny that Kashmiris created internal fault lines themselves, to be conveniently nurtured by Pakistan.

Reading Dr Manoj Joshi's *The Lost Rebellion*,[1] I found that militancy from 1989 to 1998 left about 20,000 dead, many injured and thousands traumatized. The book gives a graphic account of Kashmir in the nineties and confirms more or less whatever I had heard from friends and relatives or read in the media.

It is often assumed that Kashmiris were but a docile community that refrained from resisting authority until the start of militancy in the late eighties. Yet, history is witness to failed attempts by invaders to conquer our land due to stiff resistance put up by our forefathers. However, successive rule of Kashmir by the Mughals, Afghans, Sikhs and Dogras shaped our response to conquerors who tried to bring Kashmir under their control.

One of the main reasons that Pakistan adopted guerrilla warfare techniques was its sense of military inferiority, as compared to India. Since it cannot compete militarily with India in conventional warfare, it has aligned with militarily superior countries such as the US and China. Pakistan learnt 'proactive, even pre-emptive' strategy from the US that enables it to face and combat a large and implacable Indian army as detailed by Stephen Philip Cohen in his book, *The Idea of Pakistan*.

Pakistan learnt the technique of guerrilla warfare and people's war from the US, beginning with a special forces unit set up with the help of the US in 1959. Pakistan also probed deeper into the idea of developing a slow and inexpensive strategy of warfare as a viable alternative to conventional war. It studied various countries such as Algeria, Yugoslavia, north Vietnam and China. Although the low-cost war was thought to be relevant to Kashmir, such techniques did not prove successful in the war of 1947–48, 1965 (Indo-Pak war) and 1971 (Bangladesh liberation). However, from 1980 to 1989, the Pakistan army succeeded in its joint attempt with the US to compel the Soviet Union to withdraw from Afghanistan. Emboldened by its success, Pakistan tried the technique of 'people's war' in supporting the Sikh separatists during the Khalistan movement in India in 1984, but that did not create much of an impact. In 1989, however, Pakistan was successful in fuelling a major rebellion in Kashmir, now known as 'Islamic insurgency' and 'terrorism'.

In the years following Pakistan's humiliating defeat at the hands of India in the Bangladesh Liberation War of 1971, American professional dominance in the Pakistani army began to wane. As a result of the 1971 debacle, the Pakistani army became disillusioned with Americans. It was Zia-ul-Haq, an army officer, who initiated a process of 'reprofessionalization' of the army. One of the reasons for initiating a proxy war in Kashmir was to avenge its defeat in the Bangladesh Liberation War. Every staff officer who passes out from the Pakistan Military Academy

(PMA) expresses his commitment to avenging the 1971 war defeat during the oath-taking ceremony.

ISLAMIZATION OF THE PAKISTAN ARMY

General Zia-ul-Haq's tenure was also a period of growing 'Islamic' orientation of the army. Islamic teachings were introduced as part of the curriculum at the military Staff College. Further, in seeking strategic direction from the Islamic guidance, Pakistan accorded an important position to terror. International security expert Stephen Philip Cohen's research[2] revealed that the Pakistani military officers considered terror to be a legitimate instrument of state power if it was sanctioned by the Quran. According to the officers, a strategy that failed to strike terror in the hearts of its enemy was bound to fail. Therefore, terror is an essential weapon to be used in both nuclear and conventional warfare. Terror as an effective weapon of warfare has led to covert Pakistani support for militant groups operating in Kashmir and India itself.

While Zia-ul-Haq marginalized American influence, he took care to retain some of the American techniques. Thus, he revived and legitimized covert and low-intensity warfare with greater vigour than before. Whatever Cohen states is an objective assessment of the role of the Pakistani army. However, one cannot overlook the fact that the US military and western military industry, especially Britain and France, have been part of many conflicts throughout the world. The US Congress has a serious stake in the survival and growth of its defence industry by supplying arms to help warring nations who engage in fighting endless wars.

In October 1989, I visited Kashmir for the weddings of my

younger brothers, Ravi and Vinod. We also had to perform the kah-naether ceremony of my son, Siddharth. Kah-naether is a must for every child born in Kashmiri Pandit families and is equivalent to baptism. Generally, it is done on the eleventh day after the child is born. However, if it is not done on the eleventh day, it is performed at the next auspicious ceremony in the family. Siddharth was born in Kolkata on 8 January 1985 and we could not perform the function in Kolkata as there was no panditji who knew the ritual. Hence the function was performed in Srinagar in October 1989 at the time of the marriage ceremonies of my brothers.

I asked my good friend, Sarwar, to accompany me to visit the residence of Farooq Wani and Ghulam Rasool, who lived in Maisuma, Srinagar. Farooq was a senior studying Mechanical Engineering and Ghulam was an active politician of the Indian National Congress, a Member of Legislative Council (MLC). October is perhaps the best time to go for long walks in Kashmir. So we decided to walk from Jawahar Nagar to Maisuma to hand over the invitation cards to Farooq and Ghulam. Sarwar, Farooq, Ghulam and I would often walk down the bund along the river Jhelum from Amira Kadal to beyond Zero Bridge. After returning, a cup of tea at a restaurant on Zero Bridge or coffee at the Indian Coffee House was a routine during college years. Since I visited Kashmir only once every year or two, our meetings were full of warmth, curiosity and hospitality. Everyone in Kashmir loved to hear of life outside Kashmir.

Both Farooq and Ghulam were happy to attend the reception lunch. The meeting at the Ghulam Rasool residence went on much longer than planned, for more than two hours over noon chai, or salted tea. What Ghulam shared with me was shocking. In April, the Jammu and Kashmir Liberation Group (JKLF) had decided to raise their profile by chanting slogans for azadi during Friday namaz at Jama Masjid, led by Maulvi Farooq. Yasin Malik was a top leader of JKLF who lived in the same locality, Maisuma. Ghulam told me that over 200 youth of Maisuma and the adjoining areas had crossed over to PoK for arms training.

A complete strike in Kashmir on 15 August 1989, India's Independence Day, and the celebration of Pakistan's Independence Day a day earlier, were indicators that the gains of the Indira-Sheikh Accord had melted into oblivion. The integration of Kashmiris into the Indian psyche had already met a dead end.

When I shared Ghulam's words with my family, they confirmed having heard similar rumours. Since Farooq Abdullah was a founder member of JKLF in his early days in London, many believed he had a soft corner for JKLF and might still be nursing the fructification of the dream of an independent J&K, like his father. Our neighbour, a well-known intellectual and a friend of my father, Yusuf Mohammad Teng, who was secretary (cultural affairs), told me while he was visiting us that India would leave no stone unturned to crush the rebellion, and Kashmir might have to go through an unfortunate phase that may last a few decades. Kashmiris would realize how violence is self-defeating, but it would be too late.

An active member of the Congress party, Ghulam Rasool had offers to join other political outfits, like other workers, especially the National Conference. We would love talking about principles in politics and I can count myself as an influence on him for not changing his political affiliation. He had come to represent mainstream, liberal, secular and progressive political discourse and was hence, at odds with himself to explain why youth were crossing the border to pick up arms. What I found was paining him more was that the government led by Farooq

Abdullah was sitting on a potential bomb waiting to blow up and practically doing nothing. Like Ghulam, my friend Farooq Wani also lived in Maisuma. An engineer in the Public Health Engineering department, Farooq had lost his father at a young age and supported his family of three sisters and himself on the earnings from a bus owned by him. Many times when his driver was absent, Farooq would drive the bus himself. Blue-eyed, handsome and self-driven, Farooq, too, was liberal and progressive in approach and thought.

Although I did not visit Kashmir from 1989 to 2009, I visited Jammu in 1998 for the wedding of my nephew. A very good social and family well-wisher, Ghulam Nabi Naik, who had served as an MLA as well as an IAS officer, invited me to the MLA residential quarters for lunch. I can never refuse a wazwan, as gushtaba is my favourite mutton delicacy. He surprised me by saying that I would be meeting a special old friend for lunch but kept me guessing who it would be.

Lo and behold, it was my friend, Ghulam Rasool, who was an MLC then. We exchanged pleasantries and reminisced about the old days. We remembered our last conversation in Maisuma, the long walks on the Bund, coffee sessions at the Indian Coffee House on Residency Road, Srinagar, and our pain at what had unfolded over the last ten years. It was great to see Ghulam in good health and living as a Congressman in the Valley, upholding the values dear to him.

Ghulam told me about the alleged misbehaviour of the paramilitary forces with women during house searches at Chotta Bazaar in Old City that had triggered widespread protests in Srinagar on the night of 20 January 1990. When a procession, including women, protesting the violence, reached Gawkadal, the Central Reserve Police Force (CRPF) fired at them. One of the persons who had escaped death in this firing was my friend Farooq.[3] Many years later, Farooq visited me in Mumbai and told me that he remembered having seen hundreds of people protesting at Gawkadal against the Chotta Bazar incident, when the CRPF suddenly opened fire and indiscriminately shot at them. Farooq, too, took sixteen bullets but miraculously survived after a three-hour surgery at the Shri Maharaja Hari Singh (SMHS) Hospital. Having been a primary witness, he recounted that in the Gawkadal massacre, fatalities officially reported were much below those cited by human rights groups and eyewitness accounts.

What is painful is that no action has been taken against those responsible for ordering the shooting as well as those responsible for select killings of Kashmiri Pandits.

Now a retired chief engineer, Farooq has turned into an entrepreneur and we still maintain the same friendship that we enjoyed during our college days.

A few years later, after Ghulam met me in Jammu, while visiting his in-laws in the Navpora area, near Khayyam Cinema, he was gunned down by militants.

Farooq's shooting happened on 20 January 1990, a day after the massive exodus of Kashmiri Pandits had begun. There was fear amongst the Pandits after the murder of Tika Lal Taploo, a 58-year-old advocate and leader of the Kashmir unit of the BJP, by two young men in September 1989. On 4 November 1989, N.K. Ganjoo, a retired sessions judge, was shot by three terrorists on Hari Singh Street, an extremely busy road near Lal Chowk. Farooq Abdullah had resigned from the post of chief minister on 18 January 1990, protesting against the appointment of Jagmohan as the governor.

There are varying accounts of the role of Jagmohan on assuming office in January 1990. In fact, Jagmohan was selected on the midnight of 18 January, and he was asked to take up his new assignment immediately. He left for Kashmir aboard a BSF (Border Security Force) aircraft the same day and took his oath in Jammu that evening. Both leading parties, the National Conference and the Indian National Congress, boycotted his oath-taking ceremony. He was briefed on the seriousness of the situation by northern army commander, Lieutenant General Gobinder Singh, on 19 January in Jammu. The new governor wanted to go to Srinagar on 20 January itself, but weather conditions were not favourable for air travel. The director general of police, J.N. Saxena, had arrived in the evening to brief Jagmohan but had presumably not mentioned the searches in Chotta Bazar.

Jagmohan and the police chief Ved Marwah reached Srinagar the next morning, on 21 January 1990. There seemed to be no functioning administration. It was a cold day. To reassert the authority of the state, Jagmohan formally requested the Army to help bring the situation under control.

Armed militants had begun to turn out, chanting Allahu Akbar and azadi with the conviction that azadi was just about to come. On 22 January 1990, a rumour was spread that four Jammu and Kashmir Armed Police (JKAP) constables were shot dead by the CRPF, which galvanized JKAP personnel in uniform to join the chorus. They joined the militants with their weapons, marched towards the police control room, some shouting '*Hum chahtein hain azadi*' [we want freedom]and 'Indian dogs, get out'. When Ved Marwah asked the policemen to identify those who were killed—no one knew who were killed; no one knew who had died. Thus, a major crisis was averted. 'The whole story had been concocted with a view to laying the stage for what officials say is a plan to sparkle the final uprising,' writes Manoj Joshi.[4]

Select killings of four Indian Air Force personnel at Rawalpora bus stand and the Gawkadal massacre put people at the mercy of either militants or the security forces. According to some, the JKLF's plan was to deliver a coup de grâce on 26 January 1990, a Friday. The plan was to collect a million or so people at the Eidgah prayer ground for special prayers for the 'martyrs' and conduct a dramatic 'independence' ceremony in which the Indian flag would be burnt and an 'Islamic' flag hoisted. All this would unfurl in front of foreign journalists who had been asked to come to Srinagar to witness something 'special'.

The government ordered a pre-emptive curfew from the afternoon of 25 January and enforced it with full might. For the next few months, the remaining Kashmiri Pandits, fearful for their lives, left the Valley, and curfews became a norm of daily life for many months and years thereafter.

For Kashmiris, it has been a zero sum game. A generation of Kashmiri youth has been lost chasing a dream set in motion by a leadership that regrettably lost little in physical terms. Teenagers were brainwashed and lured to take up arms training. Thirty-one camps were set up in PoK for training recruits mostly from poor and rural areas in the Valley. Some estimates suggest about 40,000 people died at the hands of militants and security forces. Thousands were injured and traumatized. The original residents of Kashmir for over 5,000 years, the Kashmiri Pandits, were driven out of their abode. Many Kashmiris did not know how to react. On the one hand, the images of an independent Kashmir seemed a compelling proposition for some, and on the other, they were too afraid to speak for their own lives or be in a position to help others. There was a lack of leadership even amongst Pandits, as they neither had a D.P. Dhar or Shiv Narayan Fotedar, a respected politician and parliamentarian, nor a tall leader and social worker like Kashyap Bandhu. The Pandits are still in search of a unifying leader. The Muslim leadership soon got fragmented into multiple groups and their actions were determined by those who supported them financially and ideologically.

Kidnappings played a key role in the era of militancy. Kidnappings, starting with that of Rubaiya Sayeed, daughter of the home minister, Mufti Mohammad Sayeed, became a means to secure the release of captured militants.

My senior, B.K. Bakshi, who retired as the chairman of the Indian Oil Corporation, has written a book[5] on the kidnapping of K. Doraiswamy who was executive director (engineering) at Indian Oil's marketing division in Mumbai. B.K. Bakshi had staked his prestige on the release of Doraiswamy. He had mobilized the whole organization, including the local dealer network of Indian Oil in the Valley, to help secure his release. Doraiswamy was released in fifty-three days by militants. The Zewan Oil terminal project, which Doraiswamy was leading, finally got commissioned in 2010, twenty years after the original plan.[6]

Ikhwanul Muslimeen, who had kidnapped Doraiswamy, had also kidnapped and killed H.L. Khera, General Manager, HMT, earlier on 6 April 1990. The same day, they had kidnapped two Muslims, the vice-chancellor of Kashmir University, Mushir-ul-Haq, and his private secretary, Abdul Ghani Zargar. They, too, were killed on 10 April. The nineties was to reveal the worst side of terrorism and incidents that would shock the conscience of every peace-loving person in the Valley. Hazratbal Mosque, the most sacred place of worship for Muslims in Srinagar, was occupied by terrorists for thirty-two days in October and November 1993. Another holy place, the mausoleum of Sheikh Nooruddin (known as Nund Rishi), was occupied by Afghan mercenary terrorist, Mast Gul, in May 1995.

Lashkar-e-Taiba, Hizbul Mujahideen, Al-Qaeda, the Taliban and other terrorist groups brought the hope of a normal life for ordinary Kashmiris to naught. Indian security forces, in their endeavour to contain terrorism, have not come out without collateral damage either. Kashmiris were at the receiving end from both sides but it is not the time now to pause and think. Have we not suffered enough? And how long will our future generations suffer in an insecure, abnormal environment?

14

CONVERT, LEAVE OR DIE
(Raliv, Tsaliv, Galiv)

'Raliv', 'tsaliv' and 'galiv' were three words in Kashmiri that my mother and grandmother would often speak about while recalling a dark phase in Kashmir's history. Raliv (convert), tsaliv (leave) or galiv (die) were used in a decree by Sikandar, the 'iconoclast' of the Shah Mir dynasty who ruled Kashmir from AD 1389 to AD 1413, ordering Pandits to convert to Islam, flee the Valley or opt to die. He had unleashed wholesale destruction on Hindu shrines, including the Martand temple. Most Pandits either converted, fled Kashmir or lost their lives. Only eleven Pandit families are reported to have survived this phase of tyranny and stayed back in the Valley.

No one could ever imagine that a day would come over five centuries later when the entire population of Kashmiri Pandits would be forced to flee the Valley in a democratic republic. 19 January 1990 has become an important day in the history of Kashmir, when Pandits began the exodus en masse. I tried to gather instances of the exodus of Kashmiri Pandits over the last 600 years and found seven phases. Appendix-I (page 164) gives the details of when they happened, under whose rule and a summary comment.

In January 1990, fear and threats after selective killings of Kashmiri Pandits had reached a crescendo. About 1,100 mosques in the Valley had slogans blaring in unison from loudspeakers that generated anxiety, panic and enormous fear among the peace-loving people.

The slogans as heard by multiple people who I spoke with were directed at creating a hostile environment for the secular, liberal and pro-Indian population in the Valley.

Two such slogans were:

Kashir banawon Pakistan, Bataw varai, Batneiw saan

[We will turn Kashmir into Pakistan along with Kashmiri Pandit women, but without their menfolk.]

People's League ka kya paigam, Fateh, Azadi aur Islam

[What is the message of People's League? Victory, freedom and Islam.]

It is ironical that the second slogan rhymed with the most popular slogan in 1947, which evoked peace and harmony amongst people and the Muslim majority, who in unison vowed to protect the minority, Kashmiri Pandits.

Sher-i-Kashmir Kya Irshad
Hindu Muslim Sikh Itihad

It was Sheikh Abdullah's call for unity amongst Hindus, Muslims and Sikhs that dominated the narrative in 1947.

Kashmiri Pandits, along with their Muslim brethren, are

the original inhabitants of Kashmir. Yet, time and again, they have borne the brunt of bigotry, witnessed their homes being raided, temples being plundered and desecrated, their sacred possessions being trampled upon, their beliefs being ridiculed and, most importantly, their hopes of clinging to their soil being crushed to pieces by successive Islamic regimes, except during the time of Zain-ul-Abidin and the Mughals, excluding the reign of Aurangzeb.

AFGHAN RULE

The Afghan rule was the worst after Sikandar. The Afghan ruler Azam Khan's repressive measures resulted in a dismal collection of revenue. The collection of Birbal Dhar, a revenue collector, fell short by a lakh of rupees from the target. Azam Khan put a hundred Qizilbash soldiers around Birbal's house to prevent his escape to Punjab. A couple of days later, he enquired his uncle, Mirza Pandit Dhar, about Birbal Dhar, checking whether Birbal was planning to escape.[7] Mirza Pandit assured Azam Khan that he had no such plans for Birbal and gave him a written bond to that effect. In the evening, Mirza Pandit encouraged his nephew to seek support from Maharaja Ranjit Singh to escape the tyranny of Afghan rule. Birbal left his wife and daughter-in-law in the house of a Muslim noble, Qudus Gojawari, and took his son Raja Kak with him.

When Azam Khan came to know about the escape of Birbal and enquired of Mirza Pandit where he had gone, the latter replied, 'Should he care no more for the world, he will go to the Ganges; otherwise he will go to Maharaja Ranjit Singh and bring Sikhs against you.'

Azam Khan asked, 'What to do then?'

Mirza Pandit replied, 'Put me to death.'

Azam Khan said, 'What about the outstanding amount against Birbal?'

Mirza Pandit replied, 'You may put them against my name.'

Azam Khan did no harm to Mirza Pandit but put a recovery amount to the tune of ₹1000 per day on him for nine days. When the son-in-law of Birbal discovered the whereabouts of Birbal's wife and daughter-in-law, he shared it with Azam Khan. The latter summoned them to Sher Garhi Palace. Birbal's wife committed suicide by consuming poison while being taken in a boat to Sher Garhi to save herself from being dishonoured, but the daughter-in-law was seized and sent to Kabul.

Birbal convinced Maharaja Ranjit Singh to liberate Kashmir from the tyranny of Afghan rule. He offered his son Raja Kak as security for any amount of loss if the maharaja's troops failed in the invasion of Kashmir. The maharaja then sent over 30,000 troops in charge of Birbal Dhar to invade Kashmir, commanded by Gulab Singh Jamwal (the founder of the royal Dogra dynasty and the first maharaja of J&K), Misr Diwan Chand, (second commander in chief of the Sikh empire), Hari Singh Nalwa (third comander in chief) and others. A battle ensued near the Pir Panjal mountains in which the Afghans were defeated.[8] Thus ended the long period of about five centuries of Muslim rule in Kashmir.

After the persecution of Kashmiri Pandits during the reign of Sikander, who forcefully converted them to Islam, dissatisfaction of the Muslims and Pandits occupying government jobs again surfaced in violent demonstrations in 1931. This has been a constant source of resentment amongst Muslims over the centuries. Kashmiri Pandits have always pursued education to gain government employment as teachers or in the administration, unlike Muslims, who were engaged in agriculture, horticulture, handicrafts, shawl-making, hospitality and other service-sector businesses. The Pandits were quick to master whatever became the official language of the rulers—Sanskrit during Hindu rule, Persian during Mughal and Afghan rule and Urdu and English during Sikh and Dogra rules, respectively.

Being Brahmins, pursuing education was ordained, as they worshipped Saraswati, the goddess of learning. Hence, it was natural for rulers to bank upon this pool of educated manpower that was proficient in the language of court and administration. It was equally natural for Muslims to see their Pandit brothers as part of the ruling establishment and hold them responsible for implementing any unpopular and inhuman decision made by rulers. The resentment would be greater during times of agrarian crisis, which used to be a constant curse of nature due to excessive rains and floods. However, due to various social initiatives taken up by the Muslim community with some support from the administration, the pursuit of formal education amongst Muslims gained greater momentum, mostly since the early part of the twentieth century.

It is now an honour for Kashmiris that the Muslim community has produced toppers in the prestigious IAS examinations and the youth is excelling in other diverse fields, overtaking the earlier record of Kashmiri Pandits. However, since the Kashmiri Pandit community is fully literate, it is still easy for some sections of Muslim public opinion in the Valley to use this as a ploy to scare educated unemployed local Muslim youth with potential job losses on the return of displaced educated Kashmiri Pandits. With the outstanding performance of the younger generation in diverse fields, resentment amongst highly educated Muslim youth may not be as pronounced, but it remains an open issue, unless meritocracy and integrity are accepted and respected as vital to sprucing up local governance by the Kashmiri polity and society.

Those Kashmiri Pandits who fled their homes in 1990 were not destined to go back any more; over twenty-five years down the line, the idea of returning to the comforts of our home and hearth still remains a distant dream.

It also marks a collective failure of secular, tolerant, peaceful and educated members of the majority community to thwart attempts by zealots in preventing the exodus of the Kashmiri Pandit minority. Alas! There was no Sheikh Mohammad Abdullah in 1990 and no slogan—'*Hindu Muslim Sikh ittehad*'. Would a non-violent satyagraha-type movement like that of 1966 by the Pandits succeed in thwarting the well-coordinated unleashing of an environment of fear and tyranny? Probably not.

It is soothing to recall this Lal Vaakh:[9]

Kus maryi ti kasuv maaran
Maryi kus tay maaran kas
Yus hari treevyith gari gari karyey
Adi su maryi tay maaran tas

[Who is to die and who can they kill?
Who can kill and who is to die?
One who forgets God for the sake of the hearth,
Is sure to die and is to be killed.]

The return of the Kashmiri Pandits of the seventh exodus after 1990 has added a new dimension to the resolution of issues in Kashmir, with the demand of a separate homeland of Union Territory status as per the Indian Constitution within the Valley. I do not know what taqdeer has in store for me but my wish is to be in a Kashmir that puts up no geographical boundary in the Valley for the movement of people of any faith, and a Valley that resounds with the preachings of Lal Ded and Nund Rishi, a Valley in which Kashmiriyat flourishes in letter and in spirit in the composite synergic culture that existed during Bud Shah's time.

15

BEYOND EXODUS AND BACKCHANNEL DIPLOMACY

Contrary to popular perception, it is not true that efforts have not been made in the past twenty-five years to resolve disputes between India and Pakistan, especially regarding Kashmir. Backchannel diplomacy had its origins in the time of Pakistani prime minister Nawaz Sharif and Indian prime minister Atal Bihari Vajpayee, when R.K. Mishra and Niaz A. Naik started negotiating the backchannel in their capacities as special envoys of their prime ministers. They were nominated after the Lahore Summit in February 1999. Mishra, a veteran journalist, was the founding chairman of the Observer Research Foundation, a leading think tank in India. Mishra was a confidante of Vajpayee and accompanied him on his famous bus journey to Lahore. On the other hand, Naik was a distinguished diplomat and former foreign secretary of Pakistan. He had also served as High Commissioner to India. It is gathered that Mishra and Naik had secretly brainstormed a solution for the Kashmir problem. The two reported directly to the two prime ministers.

With Mishra's demise and the murder of Naik in 2009, two key Track II diplomats who had laid the contours of a possible solution were no more with us. Kushanava Choudhury had managed to interview Naik in Islamabad on Track II efforts post the famous Lahore Summit of Nawaz Sharif and Vajpayee.[10]

Choudhury reported that both Naik and Mishra were in favour of discreet diplomacy for resolving the Kashmir issue, which should be equitable, feasible and implementable. Finally, it was decided that any solution had to be final and not partial. Having discussed and rejected many possibilities such as the Dixon Plan, an independent Kashmir and the Northern Ireland model, talks were terminated when the use of the river Chenab as a potential new border was brought up, and the Kargil conflict followed.

Fifteen years later, in his book, *Neither a Hawk Nor a Dove*, Khurshid Mahmud Kasuri,[11] who served as the foreign minister of Pakistan from 2002–2007, provides an insider's account of backchannel negotiations between India and Pakistan during his tenure. These covered all unresolved issues such as Siachen, Sir Creek boundary issue, water disputes and, most significantly, Kashmir. As Kasuri argues, the logic behind establishing backchannel diplomacy was to discuss the disputes in a 'confidential' manner, away from the media glare, so that a joint draft could be agreed upon by both sides and presented to their respective cabinets, parliaments, media and the public.

The backchannel diplomacy that was pursued between 2004 and 2007 was forged after the 6 January 2004 joint statement that was issued in Islamabad in the wake of talks between Pakistan president Pervez Musharraf and Indian prime minister Atal Bihari Vajpayee. The backchannel negotiators were Brijesh Mishra, national security advisor to the prime minister of India, and Tariq Aziz, secretary of the National Security Council (NSC) and confidante to Pervez Musharraf. After the Congress came to power in India under the prime ministership of Manmohan Singh, J.N. Dixit, Singh's national security advisor, assumed the role of backchannel negotiator. After Dixit's demise, Satish Lamba remained the backchannel negotiator for quite some time.

Apparently, both countries were to discuss the issues of Siachen, Sir Creek, river waters and the dispute over J&K. The resolution of the Kashmir dispute entailed meetings with Kashmiri leaders and taking their perspectives into consideration for identification of regions in Kashmir, demilitarization, self-governance and joint mechanism of specified elected members from both sides of Kashmir to meet periodically and promote travel, trade and tourism.

During backchannel negotiations, it was felt that once the outstanding issues were resolved, India and Pakistan could sign a treaty of peace, security and friendship, which would ensure lasting harmony between the two countries. Thus, it is evident that there seemed to be a broad understanding at the political level of both the countries for resolving the outstanding issues. Yet no one is willing to commit the same in public.

There is no alternative to dialogue amongst all stakeholders, each agreeing to abide by the rule of law and engage in uninterrupted and time-bound negotiations. Otherwise, the period of exodus could be infinite, and Kashmiris in the Valley would continue to suffer.

Dr Manmohan Singh on 17 November 2004 said, 'Kashmir needs prosperity with peace. But peace without dignity is meaningless.' Good words, but with little action, despite being at the helm for ten years—a decade wasted by the Government of India.

VOICE OF THE VALLEY

When I was in the fourth and fifth standards, *Wadi Ki Awaz* (Voice of the Valley) was an evening radio programme aired on Radio Kashmir mainly as propaganda against Pakistan. It was a popular programme and my siblings and our father used to listen to this Urdu programme.

Radio Kashmir had many popular programmes, like *Zoon Dabb, Bachon ki dunya*, and dramas like *Singari*. *Zoon Dabb* had captivated the attention of the entire Valley, every day, for twenty years. 'Zoon Dabb' was the name of the seven-storey teakwood office building of Bud Shah which got gutted a century later. Life used to come to a standstill when it was aired in the mornings, just like people in the rest of India would leave everything on Sundays to watch the *Ramayana* and the *Mahabharata* in the 1980s. The late Pushkar Nath Bhan, our neighbour in Jawahar Nagar, did the voice-over for the servant in *Zoon Dabb*, which raised civic and social issues that concerned citizens in everyday life. Bhan Sahib and two other radio artists of *Zoon Dabb* were awarded the Padma Shri. It must have been the first and last time that the Government of India honoured three artists of a single radio programme with the Padma Shri award.

On the other hand, there were PoK's own propaganda programmes on radio. Azad Kashmir Radio was at a frequency that was captured in every nook and corner of the Valley. I recall the famous song, '*Watan hamara, Azad Kashmir, jaan se pyara Azad Kashmir*' [Our nation, independent Kashmir, we love you more than our life, independent Kashmir.] It was quite natural to confuse between the rhetoric raised by the rival programmes to outmanoeuvre the other.

I recall, Azad Radio Kashmir used to air *Zarb e qaleen,* which was appropriately countered by the Srinagar station with *Jawabi hamla* by Nazki. Both channels claimed to have a finger on the pulse of the people.

Frankly, for many years in my childhood I was confused of my own identity as to whether J&K was a state of India or a part of Azad Kashmir, as enunciated by Radio Azad Kashmir! My paternal grandmother, having lived in Gilgit, Skardu and other places in PoK and never having crossed Banihal tunnel, never understood the reality of J&K being part of India after 1947. She would often tell people that I was studying abroad when I was schooling in Nainital!

Recent incidents in Kashmir bear testimony to the fact that impressionable minds can be moulded to subscribe to a narrative that evolves by sustained campaigning by the media and vested stakeholders. Today social media in the Valley has replaced the old method of mobilizing people by delivering fiery speeches at mosques. In May 2011, only 3 per cent of J&K had access to the Internet. Five years later, it had risen to over 27 per cent. A case in point: Burhan Wani leveraged the Internet as a potential tool of communication, and so did others.

Writers Aurel Stein and Walter Lawrence also referred to a peculiar trait of Kashmiris, calling it our favourite pastime—'rumour-mongering'. It is as old as our culture. Most Kashmiris would refer to the Khabr-i-Zaina Kadal as the source of rumour-mongering during my stay in the Valley. Zaina Kadal is the fourth bridge on the river Jhelum in Srinagar. It is a magnificient ancient wooden bridge made over 600 years ago by Zain-ul-Abidin, popularly known as Bud Shah, around 1427. This bridge was the hub of the city when constructed, as it was the centre of all wholesale trade. It connects Bohri Kadal with the Nawab Bazaar area. I have fond memories of going by boat from Ganpatyar to

Ali Kadal under the bridge to see my mother's aunt.

All rumours are said to have originated from this bridge, spreading through word of mouth like wildfire through the Valley. With the advent of the Internet, technology has enabled faster dissemination of information, both positive and negative. One can see innumerable local-run websites like Gulistan News, Greater Kashmir, 92.7 Big FM Srinagar, and News Wire to get a 360-degree insight into the voice of the Valley.

Today when news of the imposition of 'curfew' and 'shoot at sight' gets discussed on TV channels in India day in and day out, I laugh it away. Curfews have been part of life in Kashmir from as far back as I can recall!

When my sister was married on 5 October 1967, the baraat was expected to arrive at our residence in the evening. Dinanathji, the priest who was performing the religious ceremony, lived nearby in Jawahar Nagar but the groom and his relatives lived in the downtown area. With great difficulty, my brother-in-law with some close relatives managed to get curfew passes and reach the house of a relative in Jawahar Nagar. There was a prevailing guest control order restricting the total number of dishes to about five, and persons to about fifty. I stood at the gate to count the number of people in the marriage party with the groom. And they were only seven, including the groom, just because the Valley was under curfew.

SOCIAL MEDIA AND PERCEPTIONS

These days different points of views are frequently exchanged on social media. These can give a snapshot of various shades of opinions and views held by people who are unable to voice them on the ground. I tracked some exchanges from September

2016 and April 2017 on Facebook. Such exchanges perhaps capture the mood of the people as today's *Waadi ki Awaaz*. They indicate people's perceptions and thinking, especially of concerned civil society members like activists, educationists, engineers, doctors, journalists, students, businessmen, militants and others.

Here is the exchange of some of my friends from the Valley on Facebook. The names of the respondents have been changed to maintain anonymity.

POST 1

MAJID

The two neighbouring countries should believe in coexistence and cooperation. War in the region will be disastrous for all the people. Someone should come to the fore and try to bridge the differences. In the 1950s, '60s and '70s we had great people, with great statesmanship. They would influence public opinion. In spite of them being around, the two countries did fight wars. Nobody can deny that. But still people would see a light in those inspiring personalities. Now we have no one like them. God forbid, if the bitterness increases, it will be depressing, with no hope around. Let sense prevail. Let discretion and wisdom be given a chance.

COMMENTS

Sultan: The problem is that India, having been enslaved by Britain for years, has unfortunately, as a part of withdrawal after Independence, made the psyche of its people distorted such that the language of friendship is taken as a weakness. Power has gone to the head and aggression has become a norm towards apparently weaker neighbours.

Qurrat: Times have changed. The mediocre are ruling the roost with no vision and conviction. Statesmanship is a story of the past. Failure on the domestic front leads to jingoism and warmongering and appeasing masses.

Maqsood: These two countries were created by the British to fight as a revenge for India having fought against them. We Kashmiris have unnecessarily been caught in the crossfire. Let them leave us alone and let them fight each other if better sense prevails.

Altaf: In America hundreds of people were jailed for criticizing the war. Socialist Eugene Debs was arrested in 1918 for ridiculing the idea that the US was a democracy when it jailed people for expressing their views. Debs played guilty to the charges…

POST 2

MAJID

Writings on Kashmir are mostly repetitive and monotonous and nothing beneficial is suggested. No doubt some articles provoke your thinking and are really superb. But these are few and far between.

COMMENTS

Tamboo: We mostly write about the problems but never provide solutions.

Masood: If your enemy is stubborn and adamant, what solutions can you think of except for a continuous struggle? The only other solution is surrender, and I am not one for that.

Nighat: We were never ascribed a thinking brain. The sufferings of today are a result of implementing the same ideology year after year, hence bringing a lot of sorrow. If we did not repeat the same pattern of thinking, maybe we will find some solution to our ongoing problems.

Syed: Who will have the courage to speak the truth about Kashmir and suggest creative steps? We are in the hands of invisible directors and planners. No one speaks their own language!

POST 3

MAJID

When big powers converge to solve an issue of a country, they ensure that not hundreds, not thousands, but lakhs of people of that country are killed as a first step. The Kashmir issue has to be resolved only by the two neighbouring countries. If China, Russia or America make Kashmir a war zone, it will only bring disaster and havoc to the region. The relations between India and Pakistan have to be friendly and peaceful. These two neighbouring countries should not fall prey to big manipulations.

COMMENTS

Mir: Absolutely! Kashmir should not become a war zone...it would be disastrous.

Qadir: Will the Kashmir imbroglio ever be solved?

Nazir: Don't worry, sir, nothing is going to happen. Kashmir is a football for India and Pakistan. They play and keep people busy. People are always watching a match between the two countries and get no time to think about the real issue. Neither of them wants that either lose or win the match; the show must go on. To hell with Kashmiris. They want the land.

Nazeer: Hatred is a vital weapon for the political classes of both the countries, and nobody is ready to lose.

There are a wide range of interesting narratives, as expected. It appears that there is a general consensus that another war between India and Pakistan will be disastrous, and is unlikely, as both nations being nuclear powers have acquired mutually assured deterrents. There is deep pain and anguish due to the absence of inspiring statesmanship. Mahatma Gandhi is still revered in the Valley, which leaves hope for the people who believe in a resolution of disputes by non-violence. Nevertheless, there is fear and anxiety due to the spread of right-wing ideology, in particular Hindutva. There is a craving for wisdom and discretion to be given a chance.

At the same time, young militants are using social media to increase their following and organize mass protests. Most of the Facebook accounts show their photographs with weapons, and undergoing training. One feels bad at seeing photographs of young boys who should be in school with guns on their shoulders instead. Hilal Dar of Baramulla with a Facebook friend list consisting of over 400 people, Dr Usman Bhai of Shopian in full battle gear, Mir Shoib wearing a Burhan Wani mask and holding a flag of Pakistan are examples of how imaging is used to keep militancy alive. Calling each other 'Tiger', 'Kashmir ki jaan', 'Kashmir ki shaan', 'Real heroes of Kashmir' and using cries of 'I love Pakistan' and 'war till freedom' to fuel militancy can be seen in most Facebook posts.

Experts agree how challenging it is to counter insurgency, which is exploiting new information and communication technology.

Often videos have captured the imagination of the youth in Kashmir, like the ones of Burhan Wani, and Sabzar Bhat asking the youth to join him and threatening police to eschew their fight against terrorists.

Four districts in south Kashmir, viz. Pulwama, Anantnag, Shopian and Kulgam have increasingly become the epicentre of the new wave of insurgency. The districts had remained relatively calm even during the height of insurgency in the 1990s.

Vinay Kaura[12] writes that for many years Syed Ali Shah Geelani and many of his staunch followers have sought to frame their struggle for azadi entirely in Islamic terms with very little success. The surge in religious symbolism has, however, been recent. And in this context, Muzaffar Hussain Baig warned that the Kashmir conflict was no longer a political but a religious tool for infecting the hearts and minds of the youth.

At the same time, it is important to recall that what Nehru called an 'informal war' has existed since the 1960s. Praveen Swami writes in his book about the informal war from the early 1960s to the mid-1960s and describes the five phases of jihad till the present times. The 1960s, the second phase of jihad, acquired greater momentum and structure. Led by a master cell,[13] this phase was intended to create conditions for mass rebellion. After the master cell was eliminated by Indian counterintelligence, a third phase of jihad was unleashed by Al-Fatah, a group that thrived up to the time of the liberation of Bangladesh. After Al-Fatah, too, failed, its cadre formed the National Liberation Front, which began the fourth phase of jihad. The events witnessed since 1989–90 are a consequence of the fifth phase of jihad fought under the threat of nuclear weapons.

Statistics say there are 3 lakh security personnel deployed in the Valley, of which about 1 lakh are to guard borders against external aggression. If one looks at history and the forces deployed by the Mughals and the Afghans to maintain peace and normalcy in Kashmir, it becomes apparent that deployment of a large number of soldiers to the border seems to have been the norm ever since the fall of the Shah Mir dynasty.

Kashmir has had an increase in population from 2 lakh people in 1835 to about 12 lakh in 1921. Assuming that the population was up to 4 lakhs during the reign of the Mughals and the Afghans, the deployment of 92,400 soldiers in the Valley by the Mughals and 20,000 by the Afghans was excessive as well. The Sikh garrison in the Valley was lower.[14] It consisted of two regiments of infantry, of some 1,200 or 1,400 men. The martial spirit of the Kashmiris was originally killed by the Mughals, who had to face tough resistance from the Kashmiri soldiers during their several attempts to occupy the Valley.

The question is, who will bell the cat, and how do we catalyse this dormant goodwill yearning for a return to non-violent means for the resolution of our problems? And what is the problem? How deep is our collective understanding of the real issues at hand? Besides easy information on the Internet, another key factor responsible for growing Islamic radicalization has been the decrease in the practice of Sufi Islam, the traditional form of religious practice in this region, and the growing congregations of the Wahhabi ideology.

The generation at the forefront of agitation comprises youth mostly born after 1989. They have seen militancy, disorder and curtailment of civil liberties in their growing-up years. How much of it is due to the existence of the Armed Forces Special Power Act (AFSPA) may be debatable, but the sheer presence of troops and tanks on the roads, with the imposition of curfew by authorities or others, affects the psyche of children and the youth.

The Kashmir conflict has been understood as merely an India-Pakistan issue, when it has so much to do with relational aspects, including China, religious coexistence, tolerance and Kashmiriyat; it also has related regional, provincial and identity dimensions.

When I interacted with a host of friends who have held senior positions in the state government, a mix of educated youth who have acquired professional degrees from outside Kashmir, I got the sense that during 2017, my last visit to the Valley, there was greater unrest in south Kashmir, unlike north Kashmir during the earlier phase of militancy. Dissent was led mostly by the educated youth, unlike the uneducated youth who led the first phase post training in PoK. Many suspected active and financial support to dissent by local politicians, including the Hurriyat. An urban-versus-rural divide has emerged, affecting the income of people engaged in tourism in urban areas and other centres of tourist attraction.

Many youngsters bubbling with entrepreneurial drive, who floated enterprises in the Valley after returning with professional degrees from outside Kashmir, were strained due to cash-flow problems following closure of their units due to frequent strikes and hartals. Those who started restaurants and other allied service-sector enterprises were severely affected due to a drop in the number of tourists.

Transparency and meritocracy in employment and the award of contracts is still lacking. Governance is at a low ebb, which can be gauged from the fact that it took two years to appoint a chairman of the Jammu and Kashmir Water Regulatory Authority, affecting the awarding of contracts for dredging the river Jhelum, which is necessary to prepare the Valley against the threat of floods in future.

A lot has been written about the demise of composite culture in the Valley. While there is no denying the fact that radical Islam is being supported and financed in a structured way, and the counternarrative of Kashmiriyat has weakened, there is enough evidence to support that Kashmiriyat is dormant but not dead. It will take the commitment of people wedded to the cause of composite culture to launch a sustained, structured intervention for its revival. The task is challenging since the channels of communication of politicians with the masses are almost absent due to the environment of fear and intimidation. The intelligentsia with a liberal secular outlook also finds it difficult if national and local TV channels raise the rhetoric to such levels when sensible discussions and debates become difficult.

Can we now seriously think of reviving the dominant Sufi and Shaivite discourses and move to non-violent modes for dialogue?

16

ON THE TOP OF THE DAY
(Vaarai Chuss)

If you see two Kashmiris exchanging greetings, you are sure to hear this greeting: *Vaarai chuss.* It is perhaps the most common greeting used by Kashmiris. Its near equivalents in Punjabi (*changa hain*), Gujarati (*maje ma*) and Bengali (*bhalo aachi*) convey that a person is happy, but *vaarai chuss* is much deeper in intent, with happiness related to spiritual peace. I tried to trace the origin of this greeting, as, irrespective of our physical, mental or financial condition, we always express happiness in greetings that 'I am okay, all is well'. The nearest meaning that I got was from a noted scholar, Subhash Kak. His best guess is that *vaarai chuss* means 'I am on top of the day'. 'Vaarai' comes from 'vaar', meaning day, and 'chuss' means 'am'. Both are of Sanskrit origin. Thus the word expresses positivity—we like to believe we are on 'top of the day', irrespective of how we feel in reality—sad or happy—or how our economic condition is. The basic doctrine that defines Kashmiri culture starts with the greeting itself: *Vaarai chuss!* In adversity or prosperity, we express our gratitude and thank the Almighty as we believe we are all as well as he wishes us to be.

Many intellectuals and political leaders are right in stating that we are misleading ourselves, and the political leadership has played an active role in perpetuating myths. At all stages, they have heightened our aspiration to levels that are not in sync with the ground realities. Undoubtedly, unemployment of the educated youth and lack of economic opportunities need proper and immediate attention. The reality is that we are not endowed with mineral resources and are land-locked. Hydel power, tourism and handicrafts are our major sources of revenue, whose full potential is yet to be exploited.

But our leaders seem to have convinced us that 'you are ok, I am not ok', with respect to our overall well-being. To dream and aim for a better life and future should be everyone's right, irrespective of nationality, caste, creed, religion or colour. However, it makes sense at times to pause and study how we compare ourselves with others in our neighbourhood.

Surely one does not need a lot of data to support the premise that we are better off than our brethren in PoK. Many people who crossed over to get trained and returned from across the border have seen with their own eyes that we are way ahead where infrastructure is concerned, in the fields of education, health and governance processes. It is important to see how we compare with other states in India as well.

ECONOMICS VERSUS EMOTIONS

Noted economist Dr Jean Drèze and Nobel laureate Dr Amartya Sen in their book, *An Uncertain Glory—India and its Contradictions*,[15] have compared selected indicators for major

Indian states. Some of the indicators from the book on India are as follows:

The rural versus urban poverty ratio of J&K is seen at 8.1:12.8, as compared to the Indian national average of 33.8:20.9. The overall poverty ratio is seen at 9.4, as against 29.8. We are much better off than all states in India, except Himachal Pradesh, in poverty estimates.

The percentage of population in J&K which falls in India's lowest wealth quintile is estimated at 2.8 per cent as compared to 20 per cent in India. Only Punjab and Himachal Pradesh score better than Kashmir.

The life expectancy of 71.1 years for females and 69.2 years for males in Kashmir is better than the national average of 67.7 years for females and 64.6 years for males.

92.2 per cent of Kashmir's female population has completed five years of schooling and 68.1 per cent has completed eight years of schooling as compared to a national average of 83.7 per cent and 55.9 per cent respectively. Corresponding figures for males are 94.4 per cent and 68.2 per cent. The challenge is to provide employment opportunities to this educated segment of society.

We also come out better than the national average and other state levels for nutrition-related indicators, child health, health facilities and other public services.

Where we do not score well is our voter turnout in national elections and the representation of women in Parliament. We also tend to have a higher proportion of MPs from political dynasties as compared to the national average.

It would be wise of our politicians to share such facts with our people, especially the youth, rather than espouse anger and remorse. It is a fact that we have inequality in our society.

Inequality of income has become accentuated in J&K despite a growth in GDP. This story is, however, not different in other states in India, where 1 per cent of the people control 58.4 per cent of wealth and 10 per cent of the people control 80.7 per cent of the wealth. India's Gini coefficient, a measure of the extent of inequality, increased to 51 by 2013, from 45 in 1990. This can be attributed to the rising inequality between the urban and the rural areas, as well as within urban areas.

Politicians in Kashmir, instead of emphasizing this reality and the need for creative solutions to address this problem, have often made an emotive issue of the economic development which has caused social tension and led to pressure on the state government. It has created a 'sense of entitlement' and nurtured a lobby of stakeholders for exploiting an economic issue as an emotive one.

Politicians should also work to address issues that can boost investment in the state. The National Council of Applied Economic Research (NCAER) states that Invest Potential Index (N-SIPI 2016) has interesting takeaway points for the state and central governments. This report provides a single composite investment rating of how the twenty-nine Indian states and the Union Territory of Delhi are positioned to encourage and attract investment.

The NCAER's Invest Potential Index (N-SIPI) is constructed under five broad pillars that can be classified under four broad categories—factor-driven (labour), efficiency-driven (infrastructure), growth-driven (economic climate; and political stability and governance) and perception-driven (response to surveys).

J&K is included in N-SIPI-30 rankings, which gives data on all pillars, except perception. J&K is grouped under the sixth (bottom-most) group based on its overall ranking of N-SIPI-30 states, along with Bihar, Manipur, Jharkhand and Arunachal Pradesh. One of the main impediments to the development of J&K as an investment destination, apart from being a conflict zone, is its poor connectivity by rail and road. In addition, security concerns always loom large.

The state has only two ITIs, the fewest in any state. It is ranked 20 on overall labour score amongst thirty states. However, when it comes to infrastructure, it is ranked at the bottom, at number 30. Road density, poor Information and Communications Technology (ICT) readiness, rail density and availability of net annual groundwater are impediments for improving attractiveness for investment.

The state ranks 27 amongst thirty in stalled projects due to land-related issues and 28 in e-governance. It is ranked at 25 in overall governance, political and economy rankings.

The overall fiscal liabilities of the state stood at ₹48,314 crore on 31 March 2015. Per capita liability signifies rising debt burden on the state and individuals. Expressing concern over rising debt, the last Comptroller and Auditor General of India (CAG) report said that the percentage debt increased from 51.2 per cent to 54.95 per cent of the Gross State Domestic Product, at the end of 2014–15, as compared to 2013–14. At the end of 2014–15, the accumulated liabilities were 1.67 times the government's revenue receipts during 2014–15, and 5.81 times the government's own tax and non-tax revenues during 2014–15.

Political and bureaucratic commitment at all levels is required to make a behavioural and administrative transformation. I am reminded of a conversation with some senior corporate executives in Mumbai in October 2012 as to why investors were avoiding J&K. Rahul Gandhi, current president of the Indian National

Congress, had reached out to India's corporate and industrial luminaries—Ratan Tata, Kumar Mangalam Birla, Deepak Parekh, Rajeev Bajaj and others—who had responded positively and accompanied him to Srinagar. He had connected well with the youth when he said, 'One of the first things which you need to have is stability, and you also need to have trust. You will find that things will start moving once there is trust.'

A friend of mine had narrated an anecdote on duplicity to me. While researching for this book, I found the same written by D.D. Thakur in his book, *My Life: Years at the Bar, Bench and in Kashmir Politics*. Mohammad Amin, an IAS officer, was the finance secretary under D.D. Thakur. To promote investment in industry in J&K, Sheikh Abdullah had ordered a refund of sales tax on goods produced in the state by industrialists from Mumbai. This was a continuation of the policy enacted by Mir Qasim in 1971. However, after the death of Sheikh Abdullah, Farooq Abdullah seems to have directed Mohammad Amin against releasing the refund amount. Naturally, industrialists were agitated and complained against the finance secretary to Farooq Abdullah. Thakur writes that Farooq Abdullah gave two contradictory sets of instructions—one in English and one in Kashmiri.[16] But one of the senior executives with the industrialists, who was a Kashmiri Pandit, saw through the ruse and eventually informed the others about the real meaning of the instruction given in Kashmiri!

In the recent past, many people have recalled how Kashmir was an integral part of the historical Silk Route. The China-Pakistan Economic Corridor (CPEC) is a massive development programme of $46 billion. The road network entails the linking of Gwadar Port to Kashgar in China's restive Xinjiang region through three alignments—the eastern, central and western highways. In addition, the multimodal, multidimensional corridor will comprise of rail links, oil and gas pipelines, and an optical fibre link. A 2,700-km highway shall link Kashgar to Gwadar through the Khunjerab Pass and the Karachi-Lahore Motorway. CPEC also links Xinjiang with Gilgit-Baltistan and Khyber Pakhtunkhwa. Connecting up Kashmir with CPEC makes an interesting proposition to pursue after addressing Indian concerns on sovereignty and territorial integrity.

A recent study by the World Bank group, 'Glass Half Full— the Promise of Regional Trade in South Asia' has estimated a potential trade of $37 billion per year from an actual trade of about $2 billion if all barriers to trade are removed and mutual trust is restored between India and Pakistan.

Truly, Kashmir can also become a corridor for the flow of trade and energy for south and Central Asia and beyond. Iran, Turkmenistan, Kyrgyzstan, Uzbekistan and even Russia can be sources of supply for natural gas. The IPI gas pipeline can become a peace pipeline. Turkmenistan, Afghanistan, Pakistan, India gas pipeline (TAPI) can become UTAPI, KUTAPI and RUKTAPI and then ARUKUTAPI, connecting Uzbekistan, Kazakhstan, Russia and Azerbaijan as proposed by Mani Shankar Aiyar, former petroleum minister of India, depending on the political will of the people in the subcontinent.[17]

Three decades of turmoil have resulted in various psychiatric illnesses and psycho-social distrurbances, both in people in the Valley and amongst those who have migrated outside Kashmir. Depressing statistics are appearing in the media. As per the United Nations Drug Control Programme (UNDCP), there are around 70,000 people addicted to drugs in the Kashmir Valley, including 4,000 women and girls.[18] S.A. Bhat and N. Imtiaz, in an article, have quoted a study by Dr M.A. Maqgoob and K. Dutta that there are around 2.11 lakh drug addicts in the Valley.[19] Drug menace is becoming a greater threat for future generations, and many studies indicate conflict and unemployment as the main reason.

In tandem with economic growth, becoming a centre of excellence for 'scientific humanism' as espoused by our composite culture could create opportunities for educationists, scholars and researchers to revive the educational spiritual space and address the global problems of growing intolerance. Propagating the synergic culture of Kashmir can become a global social and entrepreneurial initiative. Of course, it assumes that the state shall opt to favour Sufism over Salafism as the primary doctrine to live in harmony with those who believe in composite culture and Shaivite and Buddhist beliefs.

The conditions precedent for attracting investment for growth, beyond tourism and handicrafts, is peace, security and harmony.

17

MULTIDIMENSIONAL DISPUTE

What really strikes me about the extant literature on Kashmir is the centrality given to the legality of the Kashmir dispute. The events outlined are those that took place from 1947. While legality is certainly one of the integral components of the dispute, I feel it is only the tip of the iceberg and that there are many other elements that have also potentially contributed to the continuance of the dispute. Considering all these elements, I feel that the Kashmir dispute has a 'LeLaMOKSHI' dimension. To put it more clearly, 'Le' stands for legality, 'La' for land, M for morality, O for operationality, K for Kashmiriyat, S for Sufism, H for historicity and I for identity. These elements have to be understood separately while also being studied in conjunction with each other as they are not mutually exclusive. In outlining the contours of 'LeLaMOKSHI', I am inspired by Alastair Lamb,[20] who offered explanations and reasons for the Kashmir problem in his book titled, *Crisis in Kashmir: 1947-1966*, saying it involves the struggle between the medieval Islamic theocracy of Pakistan and the modern secular state of India, and there has been much in evidence in Pakistani political thought that distresses the image of a secular Indian democracy.

Since I have already explained historicity, morality, Kashmiriyat and Sufism, I will address the remaining elements individually.

LEGALITY

When British rule ended in India in August 1947, the princely states were left to choose whether to join India or Pakistan or to remain independent. Kashmir was the largest princely state of India. While most of the 562 Indian princely states, barring Junagarh, Hyderabad and J&K, had made up their mind to join either India or Pakistan before 15 August 1947, the inability of Maharaja Hari Singh to take a final call before that day left J&K open to exercising any of the three options.

Being a Hindu ruler of the only predominantly Muslim majority state may have made the decision difficult for him. He offered a 'standstill agreement' to both Pakistan and India to gain some time to decide. Pakistan signed the agreement but India sought some clarifications and did not sign it. On 11 August 1947, prime minister Ram Chand Kak, who seemingly advocated independence or favoured accession to Pakistan, Kashmir being a Muslim-majority state, was dismissed by the maharaja. Mohammad Ali Jinnah, in July 1947, had written to the maharaja promising 'every sort of favourable treatment', and lobbied with Ram Chand Kak, through leaders of Jinnah's Muslim League party.

The maharaja was well aware of Sheikh Abdullah's preference for aligning with secular India and his lack of faith in the two-nation theory. The indecision of the maharaja became an excuse for Pakistan to capture Kashmir by force. An armed insurgency in

Poonch and the tribal invasion from Uri were set in motion aided by Pakistan. According to Christopher Snedden, an Australian political scientist, Jammu Muslims, too, joined the uprising in Poonch and the western districts of J&K and instigated the formation of the Azad Kashmir government under the leadership of Sardar Ibrahim, a Muslim Conference party leader. They took control of most of the western part of the state by 22 October, and on 24 October 1947, they formed the Azad Kashmir (free Kashmir) government, based in Pallandri.[21]

The maharaja's troops, heavily outnumbered, had limited resources to face the tribal and planned army invasion in J&K. The Government of India received a desperate appeal for help from the maharaja on the evening of 25 October.

The Government of India decided to send V.P. Menon to Jammu to meet the maharaja, who was ready to accede at once. With the signed copy of the instrument of accession and a letter describing the plight of the state and reiterating the request for military help, Menon flew back to Delhi. There was a long discussion, and it was decided that the accession of J&K should be accepted, subject to the provision that a plebiscite would be held in the state when the law and order situation allowed. The decision had the fullest support of Sheikh Abdullah.

The maharaja wrote in a letter, 'I wanted to take time to decide to which dominion I should accede, whether it is not in the best interest of both the dominions and my state to stand independent, of course, with friendly and cordial relations with both... With the condition in my state at present and the great emergency of the situation as it exists, I have no option but to ask for help from the Indian dominion. Naturally, they cannot send the help asked for by me without my state acceding to the Dominion of India. I have, accordingly, decided to do so, and I attach the Instrument of Accession for acceptance by your government. The other alternative is to leave my state and my people to freebooters.'

Lord Mountbatten in his reply[22] on 27 October 1947, accepted the Instrument of Accession, stating, 'In the special circumstances, Highness, my government has decided to accept the accession of Kashmir state to the Dominion of India and it is my government's wish that as soon as law and order have been restored in Kashmir and her soil cleared of the invader, the question of the state accession should be settled by a reference to the people.'

Notwithstanding the legal documentation backing the accession of Kashmir to India, it is important to recall what Nehru, while addressing the Parliament on 7 August 1952, stressed—that questions regarding the future of J&K could be decided only by the people of the state, and hence the surrounding politics should be fashioned in accordance with this.

The Indian government, thus, had legal possession of J&K. Thereafter, the duly elected constituent assembly of J&K ratified accession to India.

LAND

Kashmir constitutes the northernmost state of the Republic of India, occupying an area of 222,236 square kilometres. The state was divided into three regions at the time of accession to India in October 1947.

a) The outer hills and the middle mountains of the Jammu division, consisting of Udhampur, Jammu, Reasi, Mirpur and Poonch.

b) The Kashmir province, consisting of the Kashmir Valley and the Muzaffarabad district.

c) The far side of the great watershed range, including Astor, Gilgit, Baltistan and Ladakh.

The total area of J&K is around 2,22,236 sq km. In the Kashmir region, Aksai Chin and Shaksam Valley are about 37,244 sq km, both occupied by China; Gilgit-Baltistan has an area of about 72,971 sq km and Azad Kashmir (PoK) under occupation of Pakistan has an area of around 13,297 sq km. This leaves us only the Kashmir Valley in the Kashmir region as the area under India's jurisdiction, which is approximately 16,000 sq km. India is left with the possession of only about half of the area of Kashmir as seen on a political map of India. The Pir Panjal mountains separate the Kashmir Valley from the great plains of northern India while the Himalayan range separates it from Ladakh. The Valley is about 5,300 feet above sea level. However, with a higher population of 69 lakh in Kashmir as against 53 lakh in Jammu and 3 lakh in Ladakh, Kashmir has naturally dominated the discourse on conflict resolution for the past six decades.

While Kashmir Valley is predominantly Muslim, Jammu and Ladakh are predominantly Hindu and Buddhist, respectively. If one were to take religion as the basis of accession, Jammu and Ladakh would always prefer integration with the Hindu-majority India. Territorially speaking, the size of the Valley is not large enough to be of interest to either India or Pakistan; adding incremental land to its territory should, therefore, interest neither India nor Pakistan. However, the location is strategic.

According to *The Times*, the maharaja had originally resigned to Kashmir's accession to Pakistan because of geographical contiguity and its Muslim-majority population. However, due to the leadership of Sheikh Abdullah, Muslims did not subscribe to the two-nation theory of Partition. Maharaja Hari Singh, it appears, recognized J&K's lack of connectivity with India as a major constraint for the princely state becoming a part of India. He sanctioned a scheme on 28 July 1947 for metalling Kathua Road. Kathua Road was to connect Jammu with India (then Union of India) through Pathankot, which would have been the only route of traffic between Jammu and India.

J&K was made contiguous with India after the award of four tehsils of the Gurdaspur district of Punjab to India by the Radcliffe Commission, set up to demarcate the boundary between India and Pakistan. This gave India a narrow land corridor connecting Punjab to the Kathua district of J&K. Had the four tehsils of Gurdaspur district been awarded to Pakistan based on the high population of Muslims in the district of Gurdaspur, India would not have had a reliable connectivity of rail or road with J&K.

Had J&K Muslims, who comprised 77 per cent of the population at the time of accession, been united and unequivocal in their desire for the princely state to become a part of Pakistan, Hari Singh would have had only one option—accession to Pakistan. But the sheer presence and leadership of Sheikh Abdullah tilted the scales in favour of secular India.

OPERATIONALITY

The maharaja had considered Kashmir's accession to Pakistan following the principle of geographical contiguity, economic dependence and ties of religion. His attitude may have changed when he realized that J&K Muslims led by Sheikh Abdullah supported accession to India. Awarding the Gurdaspur land corridor to India was another major development which made accession feasible.

Geographically, the only railway line that entered J&K at the time of accession was a branch of the north-western railway that connected Sialkot, some twenty-five miles away in Pakistan, to J&K's winter capital, Jammu city. J&K had few motorable roads; the main road, like railway links, connected Jammu city to Sialkot. Of the three roads to Srinagar, two entered J&K from areas that were to become part of Pakistan. The first was the all-weather Jhelum Valley Road, which ran alongside the Jhelum river for 132 of its 196 miles. This road began in Rawalpindi, where there was a railhead, and then via Murree and Domel, near Muzaffarabad, to Srinagar. A second road went from the North West Frontier Province (NWFP) rail terminus of Havelian, seventy-one miles further north of Rawalpindi, via Abbottabad to Muzaffarabad, and then to Srinagar. A third, 'more picturesque' road was an extension of the Sialkot-Jammu road. This route went for 203 miles from Jammu city to Srinagar via the Banihal Pass, which was often snowbound during winter from December to April and was 'notoriously liable to gullying and landslips'.

In terms of communications, J&K's post and telegraph links invariably followed the major roads and/or rail links that entered the princely state. These also originated in, or traversed through, areas that were to become part of Pakistan.

Economically speaking, accession to Pakistan was feasible as the J&K economy was heavily integrated with, and dependent on, areas that were to become part of the new dominion. Upto 98 per cent of the non-timber exports went via the Jhelum Valley Road. Timber was exported by floating it down the Jhelum and Chenab rivers to points downstream in (Pakistani) Punjab. Karachi enjoyed a 65 per cent freight advantage over goods sent to Bombay (now Mumbai) or Calcutta (now Kolkata). Finally, tourism was 'of vast economic importance'. With most of J&K's services and economic activities taking place with Pakistan, and given the fact that the J&K government had sought and obtained a standstill agreement just before the British departed, many Pakistanis apparently believed that J&K would, at some point in the future, accede to it. This hope, however, was false. The J&K government had openly offered the same agreement to India, but New Delhi had been non-committal.

When the Radcliffe Commission embarked on the task of demarcating the boundary between the two dominions, Lahore emerged as a bone of contention before the Boundary Commission. Lahore and Amritsar had, between them, 40 per cent of the industries of Punjab. About 205 of the factories in Lahore belonged to the Hindus, ninety-one to the Muslims, nine to the Sikhs and nine to the other communities. The Muslims of Lahore were confident that no consideration could weigh against their numbers. The non-Muslims, especially the Sikhs, were equally certain that the Boundary Commission would not ignore the economic position and their religious and historical traditions.

The assurance by the under-secretary of state for India, Arthur Henderson, to the Sikhs that the location of their religious shrines would be taken into account with 'other factors' had raised hopes in the minds of the non-Muslims that Lahore would not go out of the Hindu land. There was more focus and interest on the future of Lahore than the tehsils of Gurdaspur being awarded to India.

Eminent journalist Kuldip Nayar, who met Lord Cyril Radcliffe, says, 'Lord Radcliffe did not attach any importance to Kashmir. He was a judge in London who drew the line between

India and Pakistan to establish two separate countries. He told me many years later during an interview that he never imagined that Kashmir would assume as much importance as it did.'

Hence, pre-Independence J&K had no link with India. It was only on 28 July 1947 that the government of J&K sanctioned a scheme for metalling the Kathua Road. This decision could have been a preparatory step in the maharaja's plan of accession to India, if any. By 25 September, the government of J&K ordered the construction of a boat bridge over the river Ravi near Pathankot, thus connecting J&K to India. Parallely, the work on the construction of a new road from Jammu city to Kathua on the Jammu state border touching Gurdaspur district in east Punjab ensued. Christopher Beaumont, who was private secretary to Radcliffe, had, in his testimony, made it clear that 'no change was made in the northern Gurdaspur line and it was always proposed to be given to India.'[23] Had these developments not taken place, operationally there was little favouring accession of the state to India.

Unfortunately, Kashmir still remains unconnected by rail even after seventy years of accession to India. We had to travel to Pathankot to take the train to Kathgodam and then on to school in Nainital. It is worth recalling that the Dogra leader Maharaja Pratap Singh in 1886 had plans for extending the metre gauge railway line from Rawalpindi to Kashmir. Plans of a 175-mile-long track with a maximum gradient of 1 in 50 and curves of 400-ft radius were prepared but raising ₹3.07 crore as budgeted became a challenge. Hopefully, the railway line from Udhampur in Jammu to Srinagar will be commissioned in our lifetime. I look forward to being part of the inaugural journey.

IDENTITY AND NATIONHOOD

What is our identity? This has become an emotive issue. The question of identity is crucially linked to ideas of nationalism and the nation. There have been divergent approaches towards defining 'nationalism' and the 'nation'. I find there is little debate over the fact that nationalism precedes the nation. In other words, nationalism gives rise to the nation-state and not the other way round. Hence, it is appropriate to begin by defining the term 'nationalism'. Elie Kedourie, in his classic essay 'On Nationalism'[24] has defined it as a doctrine that 'pretends to supply a criterion for the determination of the unit of population proper to enjoy a government exclusively its own, for the legitimate exercise of power in the state, and for the right organization of a society of states'. Ernest Gellner[25] defines nationalism as 'primarily a principle which holds that the political and national unit should be congruent'. Ernest Renan defined the nation as 'a soul, a spiritual principle...a great solidarity constituted by the feeling of sacrifices made and those that one is still disposed to make. It presupposes a past but is reiterated in the present by a tangible fact: consent, the clearly expressed desire to continue a common life. A nation's existence is...a daily plebiscite, just as an individual's existence is a perpetual affirmation of life.'

However, the definition of a nation as a political construct also underscores its subjectivity and flexibility. Nations are not a 'natural, God-given way of classifying men', according to Eric Hobsbawm.[26] Rather, what nationalism does is transform 'pre-existing cultures into nations, and sometimes invent them'. Hobsbawm also considers the nation as a social entity capable of changing. He further argues that language and ethnicity cannot be the sustained basis for claiming nationhood as they are themselves shifting, ambiguous categories and therefore, 'as useless for purposes of the traveller's orientation as cloud shapes are, compared to landmarks'.

There is another school of thought that maintains that nations are neither territorially defined units of governance nor imagined entities. They are 'real' entities whose boundaries are defined by their inhabitants in cultural and ethnic terms. Thus, national identity is primordial and immutable, and cannot be altered by manipulations by the state. Nationalists evoke the image of the 'historic homeland' as 'our homeland' by recounting tales of great exploits and events in the 'ethnic past'. All this contributes to the 'politicization of ethno-national' communities. Ethno-nationalism is quite evident amongst Sikhs, Hindus and Muslims in India. In India, ancient ethnic myths and memories associated with particular sites and territories are evoked by political groups in generating a sense of national consciousness amongst the ethnic communities of Sikhs, Hindus and Muslims.

Kashmir has now become a site of contestation between proponents of territorial nationalism and ethnic nationalism. Territorial nationalism was originally the basis of conflict over the Valley between India and Pakistan. Ever since Kashmir's accession to India in 1947, both India and Pakistan have continued to lay their claims on the region as part of their respective territories. However, following the Islamist insurgency in the Kashmir Valley in 1989, the idea of nationalism was recast in a new mould that began to denote the dominance of Islamic rhetoric in the nationalist discourse. Political groups with professed religious orientation such as the Hizbul Mujahideen and Jammat-e-Islami have argued for Kashmir's accession to Pakistan by recasting Kashmiri nationalism in the Islamic mould. To add insult to injury, Indian politicians have also been laying patriotic claims over Kashmir that are less secular and more ethnic in nature. Kashmiri Pandits, driven out of the Valley in 1990, have begun demanding a homeland through Panun Kashmir, an organization of displaced Kashmiris. In the process, Kashmir's synergic culture that is proudly referred to by the Kashmiris as Kashmiriyat seems to be getting pushed to the margins of political discourse. The centuries-old secular nationalism of Kashmir is shrinking in the face of challenges posed by religious nationalism. Our future pathway shall depend on how we wish to pursue it and preserve Kashmiriyat, our composite cultural identity.

It is important to hence analyse the importance of each element of LeLaMOKSHI at the individual level and in conjunction with each other. Only then can we realize why addressing the issues at hand in Kashmir requires a different approach and understanding.

18

RE-IMAGINING THE VISION

Sahibo sat cham mi cheani
Wath meh aslich havtem
- G.M. Mehjoor

[Lord! You are my hope and trust
Lead me to the way of truth]

Recapitulating Kashmir's history that I have attempted to put down in the preceding pages, we all know that Kashmir has been ruled by kings or rulers of different faiths. Hinduism, Buddhism, Islam and Sikhism have coexisted in a symbiotic culture, post the advent of Islam about 600 years ago. Kashmir has contributed immensely to the idea of India as a pluralistic society and a united nation. King Lalitaditya (724–761 AD) of the Karkota dynasty ruled the largest empire of India from Kashmir. Some western scholars have called him the Alexander of India. We have preserved our distinct culture and identity due to the lack of physical connectivity for mass integration with mainland India and other regions bordering our state.

Hence, it is important to factor in the legality, land, morality, operationality, Kashmiriyat, Sufism, historicity and identity—all these dimensions of Kashmir. What is the type of socio-cultural-economic and political future we wish for our future generations? We need to keep in mind the contemporary world of realpolitik and the new world order, if we were to do some crystal-gazing. Let me attempt to leverage my corporate experience and look at the issue in the construct of a management discussion and analysis format, adapting some basic guidelines of strategic decision-making tools to address the issue.

There is a significant section of the Muslim population that believes accession by Maharaja Hari Singh, who vacillated in his decision to join either India or Pakistan at the time of Partition and later acceded to India, is not a final settlement of the dispute. The disputed region comprises of Jammu, the Kashmir Valley, Ladakh, northern Kashmir and PoK. However, it is also important to recognize that Jammu, Ladakh and Kashmir are three different and distinct regions with different languages, cultures and religions. Jammu, Ladakh and Kashmir came together only after the Dogra rule. It is not a state which is bound by a commonality that unifies to create a strong linkage of allegiance. The creation of J&K was a force-fit solution enforced by the British to serve their geopolitical interests mainly because of the Anglo-Russian fallout.

If we look back at the mid-fourteenth century, post the arrival of Islam, the reign of Zain-ul-Abidin (AD 1420–1470) stands out as a period when the Valley had reached its own 'Nash Equilibrium'. The Nash Equilibrium is a concept where the optimal outcome of a game is one where no player has the incentive to deviate from his chosen strategy after considering his choice of opponent. Since then, despite the early reign of the

Mughals being a period of harmony and economic prosperity, we are in a state of transition. One can assign the genesis of the problem to 16 October 1586 when Mughals set foot in Srinagar. Our yearning to attain the 'Nash Equilibrium' amongst internal stakeholders made us invite the Afghans to oust the Mughals. It also made us invite the Sikhs to oust the Afghans. One can argue that had Maqbool Sherwani not stopped Kabalis from not reaching Srinagar in 1947 before the arrival of the Indian Army, the whole of Kashmir could have become part of Pakistan. Considering the divergence of political preferences amongst people with a predominant voice supporting Sheikh Abdullah in the Valley then, it is quite possible there would have been a strong separatist section of the society wanting to firmly be with India, had Kashmir been annexed by Pakistan by force in 1947. We are still caught in the vortex of transition, and it is just a coincidence that the people's fight to oust the maharaja was running parallel to the fight of people in India against the British. The two were separate movements.

CONFLICT RESOLUTION AND GLOBAL MODELS

Firstly, we will examine some models of global conflict resolution that can help resolve the Kashmir dispute. In his book, *The Kashmir Dispute: 1947–2012 Vol. 2*, A.G. Noorani has reviewed various foreign models in depth for their applicability to the resolution of the Kashmir dispute.[27] The table below gives a compilation of global disputes, a brief description of the resolution and my understanding of each model and its relevance to the dispute in Kashmir. It is clear that there was a demand for secession, freedom, or azadi, in most cases, in most instances reviewed by me. However, it is important to note that maintaining status quo cannot resolve a dispute permanently. Reconciling sovereignty with the principle of self-determination or autonomy is possible. One can even acquire a legal but not a territorial interest in the land in the other's control. Assimilation of the people is possible without plebiscite by dialogue, goodwill, political will and statesmanship.

SIX LESSONS FROM GLOBAL DISPUTE RESOLUTION MODELS

Name of model	Dispute resolution	Key takeaways for Kashmir
Trieste-Saar model	Trieste, with a majority Slovene population, is a port city in Italy bordering Slovenia. In 1954, it was partitioned between Italy and Yugoslavia. Both, however, signed the agreement in 1975 on the border question and economic cooperation with Italy, surrendering a strip of 5 square miles to Yugoslavia. The SAARS dispute was resolved through a referendum in 1955, when Saarlanders chose Germany over France.	'Status quo' or 'business as usual' cannot resolve a dispute permanently. Political will and goodwill are necessary.

Name of model	Dispute resolution	Key takeaways for Kashmir
South Tyrol model	In the wake of the First World War, Britain and France handed over South Tyrol to Italy in 1919, despite its German-speaking majority. After twenty-eight years of negotiations, the dispute was resolved in 1992 through talks between Austria and Italy with support from South Tyrol's Representative Party (SVP). The status quo was not disturbed, but South Tyrol preserved its autonomy. Italy and Austria signed the treaty to promote cooperation across the border a year later.	Reconciling sovereignty with the principle of self-determination is possible. One can acquire a legal but not territorial interest in the land in the other's control.
Åaland Model	The Åaland Islands remained with Sweden until 1809, after which it became part of Finland. In 1919, 95 per cent of the Åalanders voted for unification with Sweden in an unofficial plebiscite. The League of Nations intervened. Finland retained sovereignty over Åaland but the islands were granted autonomy.	The settlement of a dispute on the Åaland model uses the principle of self-determination but does not entail secession. Instead, it is likely to promote a sense of fair play and justice.

Name of model	Dispute resolution	Key takeaways for Kashmir
The Irish model	Northern Ireland was colonized by the English and Scottish Protestants in the seventeenth century. The southern side was dominated by Catholics. People in the northern island were divided between joining the Republic of Ireland and remaining with the UK. Ireland and the UK displayed their political will in 1981 to form an inter-governmental council and signed an agreement in 1985 for the two parts to engage with matters relating to politcs, security and law. It paved the way for cross-border cooperation and, later, the British-Irish governments and political parties of Northern Ireland's multipartite and bilateral 'Good Friday Agreement' of 10 April 1998.	Assimilation of the people is possible while recognizing the interest of stakeholders without a plebiscite. Dialogue is the only way for countries and regions to resolve disputes. Civil wars are not a substitute.
The Quebec Model	Quebec, a large and populous province within Canada, has a majority French population who demand secession based on their distinctive culture and language. The Supreme Court of Canada successfully grappled with the issue and	One can recognize the diversity within a country rocked by separatist sentiments in a liberal manner, which Canada showed to the people of Quebec.

Name of model	Dispute resolution	Key takeaways for Kashmir
	the House of Commons passed a massive vote in 2006 recognizing the Quebecois who formed a nation within a united Canada, upholding their diversity. A referendum held earlier on sovereignty to pursue secession was also defeated.	
Aceh Accord	Aceh in Sumatra, Indonesia, was rocked by an armed secessionist movement since 1976. In 1992, violence flared up, followed by military oppression, human rights violations and growing public displeasure with the government. In 2000, the Indonesian government started negotiations with the Free Aceh Movement (Gerakan Aceh Merdeka). In 2002, they signed the Cessation of Hostilities Framework Agreement, and in 2005, they signed a more durable agreement. Aceh is autonomous in all respects, except in defence, foreign affairs, security and finance.	With the requisite diplomatic skills, statesmanship and political will, it is possible to resolve conflicts in a way acceptable to all parties undergoing dispute.

MANAGEMENT TOOLS AND THE KASHMIR DISPUTE

I have often wondered if one could get some direction for solving the Kashmir problem in the context of an India-Pakistan standoff using management decision-making tools. To solve management problems, one often falls back on Game theory. It means deployment of mathematical models of cooperation and conflict between intelligent, rational decision-makers. The applications of Game theory in economics, political science, psychology, logic, computer science, biology, politics and international relations as well as conflict resolution are well-documented. Game theory can be used to study human conflict and cooperation within a competitive situation.

The term 'game' can be misleading. Even though the concept can be used in recreational games, the concept is basically an interactive situation in which independent actors share more or less formal rules and results. The important concept of 'Game Theory' is the Nash Equilibrium, named after its inventor, John Nash, an American mathematician.

Overall, an individual can receive no incremental benefit from changing actions, assuming other players remain constant in their strategies. A game can have multiple Nash Equilibrium solutions, or none at all. When applied to the situation in Kashmir or elsewhere, it can be said that a Pareto optimality in society would be reached when minimum demands or needs of people at individual and societal level are met, where stakeholders believe in justice and generosity of the system, and conflicts in society are minimal.

Surapati Pramanik and Tapan Kumar Roy,[28] in their paper 'Game Theoretic Model to the Jammu-Kashmir Conflict Between India and Pakistan', have used a standard 2×2 Zero Sum Model to identify an optional solution. It is based on identifying the options that each country has, and an attempt to evaluate, based on a chosen option, what each of the two countries is trying to achieve.

In a similar approach, another scholar, Dr Saeed Ahmed Rid[29,] in his paper, 'Kashmir: The Prisoner's Dilemma for India and Pakistan', has applied Game Theory to establish that Pakistan and India are locked in a 'prisoner's dilemma' (PD) in Kashmir.

Unlike in the PD problem, where the value measures are around money (easily quantifiable), in the current problem, the primary value measures are pride and national identity. So, even going by PD, the preferred approach for both nations is the status quo conflict. This is better illustrated by the model created by Pramanik and Roy. While 'constructivism' or the 'multi-track diplomacy' could change the underlying emotions allowing for a change of value measures of both parties, it is doubtful that Pakistan can do that, with its 'Islamic country identity' as enumerated by Zia-ul-Haq and a biased school curriculum that almost needs to demonize India for retaining its identity.

I have developed a simple Dove-Hawk game to illustrate possible scenarios. Imagine that Dove represents politics and persons opposed to war and Hawk represents advocates and supporters of warlike policies. The numbers in the table represent the estimated value, in this case, the motivation for desirable outcomes. The players are the people and politics of India and Pakistan. Dove represents love and hawk represents hate. The numbers in the game represent hypothetical compensations.

		PAKISTAN	
I		DOVE	HAWK
N	DOVE	5, 5	-1, 10
D	HAWK	10, -1	3, 3
I			
A			

The Dove-Dove scenario would be one in which both sides agree to a bilateral solution based on the Simla Agreement. It would mean that the territory of PoK and Gilgit Baltistan would be given to Pakistan, and Kashmir, Jammu and Ladakh to India, to convert the ground reality to the de jure situation. Dove-Dove would be a cooperation-cooperation construct.

The Dove-Hawk quadrant would mean India making territorial concession (ultra Dove) and Pakistan not accepting to abide by the Simla Agreement and continuing to indulge in covert operations.

The Hawk-Dove scenario would entail India continuing to fence along the LoC or retaliating with its military might (ultra Hawk) and Pakistan agreeing to comply with the Simla Agreement.

The Hawk-Hawk scenario is more or less what is happening currently, with both sides being unable to enforce the Simla Agreement. In such a scenario, a tit-for-tat strategy is dominant.

Under this payout matrix, it is difficult to have a cooperation–cooperation, or Dove-Dove Pareto optimal solution. Nash Equilibrium is not necessarily a Pareto optimal solution. Notwithstanding our best hopes for a cooperation-cooperation or Dove-Dove framework between India and Pakistan, a bilateral solution at a country-to-country level appears difficult due to lack of trust, national pride and identity issues. Hence, we may look at a solution within the LoC in the near and medium term. BBC News Online[30] has an account of solutions and an assessment of how workable they are:

1. **Independent Kashmir.** It requires India and Pakistan to give up their existing territories. Neither will India nor Pakistan surrender the territory currently held by them. It is also unexpected of them to accept the option of plebiscite, as it could lead to Balkanization of the region. Balochistan or Sind in Pakistan could demand independence from Pakistan and so could some states in India. The situation on the ground today is radically different from what it was at the time of Independence. J&K was an independent princely state, geographically larger than sixty-eight countries of the UN and more popular than ninety. Post annexation of Azad Kashmir and Gilgit-Baltistan, the situation has changed on the ground, hence public opinion and community support neither in India nor in Pakistan would support such a course of action.

2. **Kashmir joins India.** In October 1947, Maharaja Hari Singh signed an Instrument of Accession, making J&K a sovereign part of India. While Pakistan occupied the northern areas militarily in 1948, it is unlikely today for Azad Kashmir and all northern areas to be part of India. Hence, despite the rhetoric, the reality is that what is with Pakistan will remain with Pakistan and what is with India will remain with India.

3. **Kashmir joins Pakistan.** Jammu and Ladakh are Hindu- and Buddhist-dominated areas respectively, and have shown preference for full integration within India

by abrogating Article 370. People in Jammu and Ladakh are culturally, religiously and ethnically diverse from the people of Kashmir and do not want to join Pakistan.

4. **The Chenab formula.** It envisages dividing Kashmir along the line of the river Chenab, whereby the entire Valley and Muslim- majority areas of Jammu goes to Pakistan, which gets the vast majority of land. India gets only 3,000 sq km out of 24,000 sq km. This is a clear no-no for India and hence, not practical or debatable.

5. **Independent Kashmir Valley.** Kashmir Valley is an area of 1,800 sq miles—80 miles long and over 20-22 miles wide. While the Valley sustains itself on tourism, handicrafts and agriculture, it is landlocked, and a major part of it is cut off from the rest of the country in winter. While greater autonomy and joint protectorate seems a possibility, it is inconceivable to expect India or Pakistan to support an independent Kashmir Valley.

6. **An independent smaller Kashmir.** It would mean the northern areas would remain in Pakistan, and Jammu and Ladakh would be integrated with India. Azad Kashmir administered by Pakistan and Kashmir under Indian jurisdiction would be required to merge and become an independent Kashmir. Both countries are unlikely to support it, and Pakistan more vehemently so, because it would lose access to water from the Mangala Reservoir of Azad Kashmir. While trade may continue between the two parts of Kashmir, it is important to recognize that the two parts are socially, culturally and linguistically diverse. It will pose immense challenges of social integration, especially because of the Jhelum river.

7. **Status quo.** It would mean that Pakistan retains Azad

Kashmir and the northern areas whereas India retains the Valley, Jammu and Ladakh. Many people have indicated a general understanding at the highest levels between the two countries for accepting the above reality as fait accompli. This is what was agreed in 1972 in Simla. However, a lot will need to be done to address the LeLaMOKSHI dimension to make it a workable solution.

It is also important to realize that the Pakistan government is unlikely to let go of any portion of PoK. The Pakistan military, which acts independently of the government to a certain extent, is keen on occupying India-governed J&K as well. The population of PoK wants an amicable living environment with the entire region united. However, Kashmir remains a unifying factor at the national level in Pakistan. Also, on the Indian side, the Indian government will not consider even a 'middle ground' solution, given the sensitivity attached to the perception of 'buckling', and directly impacting the vote banks at an overall country level. The state government of J&K has a largely political interest. Support depends upon the solution arrived at. The J&K population is desirous of an amicable living environment, with the entire region remaining united. However, there are emerging voices in Jammu and Ladakh for full integration within India and the abrogation of Article 370.

Hence, it is difficult to find a common solution for the entire region as a whole, given the varying interests of various stakeholders. We have to look at some of the possible measures that we can explore within the LoC with India.

For working with the LoC, we need to evaluate reforms/decisions required to be taken across some key areas. These would cover the status of Article 370: temporary versus permanent, and the scope of Article 370: level of autonomy and merging Jammu and/or Kashmir with the Union of India by the abrogation of Article 370.

Based on the identified intervention areas, the following set of alternatives can emerge:

Alternatives	Status of Article 370	Scope of Article 370	Status of J&K
Status Quo	No change	No change	No change
'One' India	Cancelled	Cancelled	Constitutionally integrate J&K fully into the Union of India
'Deemed' nation	Permanent	Devolve significant autonomy with only defence and foreign affairs under central powers	No change
'Middle' ground	Temporary with an eventual vision of integration	Limited to Kashmir	Make Jammu and Ladakh independent states of India. Kashmir Valley to remain separate, with greater autonomy.

Alternatives	Status of Article 370	Scope of Article 370	Status of J&K
'Cultural' integration	Permanent for Kashmir	Limited to Kashmir	Make Jammu and Ladakh independent states of India. Kashmir Valley and PoK to be jointly administered

Given the interest of stakeholders and their preferences, one can look at validating each of the solution ideas on the following value metrics:

- Alignment with political party preferences
  - State political parties
  - NDA alliance preferences
  - UPA alliance preferences
- Alignment with the local population's interest
- National security
- Ease of implementation

If each alternative is ranked on a scale of 1 to 5 (with 1 being least preferred and 5 being most preferred) on each of the above value metrics by the jury method, the resulting table may appear as follows:

| Alternative | Alignment | | | Alignment with local population's interests | National security | Ease of implem-entation |
	Alignment with NDA alliance	Alignment with UPA alliance	Alignment with state political interests			
Status quo	3	4	3	1	4	5
'One' India	5	5	1	2	5	2
'Deemed' nation	2	2	5	4	2	3
'Middle' ground	4	3	4	3	3	4
'Cultural' integration	1	1	2	5	1	1

We can give equal weightage to each of the four value metrics to develop a consolidated score for each of the ideas. The highest score means it is the most preferred idea, after considering the full range of preferences of the various stakeholders. The table below provides the consolidated score for each idea and highlights that the 'middle' ground emerges as the most preferred idea for debate.

Sr. No.	Idea	Weighed Average Score (higher score implies greater acceptance)
1	Status Quo	3.08
2	'One' India	3.17
3	'Deemed' nation	2.83
4	'Middle' ground	3.42
5	'Cultural' integration	2.00

Hence we can argue that moving towards the middle ground is the preferred option for solving the Kashmir imbroglio. Building peace and prosperity in J&K will also enhance India's bargaining position for any future dialogue with Pakistan on the undivided Kashmir issue. It is quite a coincidence that the middle ground scenario is consistent with a possibility that was foreseen by Dr Shyama Prasad Mukherjee in the Parliament while speaking on the motion regarding Kashmir on 7 August 1952. He said that people of the territory would have to decide the two separate entities, indicating Ladakh and Jammu, could be historically or otherwise be made a part of India. He did not rule out autonomy for Kashmir.[31]

Self rule as sought by the People's Democratic Party (PDP) and autonomy as demanded by National Conference also seek devolution and de-centralization of governance to address the issue of Kashmiri identity and the LeLaMOKSHI dimension.

Almost seventy years after Partition, India and Pakistan do not seem eager to initiate a serious peace process. Both have compelling motives to seek a resolution to the dispute, albeit driven by different rationales. India harbours the aspiration of becoming a global power. However with an unresolved, festering dispute on its turf that causes frequent diplomatic embarrassment and consumes enormous human and financial resources, India's global aspiration is likely to be affected. Therefore, a speedy but effective resolution of the Kashmir dispute will liberate India of the mammoth task of deploying enormous resources year after year for security and counter-insurgency operation purposes. Moreover, resolution of the Kashmir dispute will bolster India's global image as a vibrant democracy and growing economic power.

Noted scholar Dr Sumit Ganguly in his book, *The Crisis in Kashmir: Portents of War, Hopes of Peace* has evaluated various options like ethnic flooding, the mailed fist strategy, some impractical options conceding the Valley, shared sovereignty holding plebiscite, independence and the protectorate option. He considers it unlikely for any government in India to concede Kashmir because it would instigate riots in the country and also because it would be detrimental to the rest of the country's Muslim population (as Kashmir is the only Muslim-majority state in the country).

The Indian state has demonstrated considerable resilience in handling insurgencies. Even today, its coercive power remains considerable. In the absence of a viable alternative strategy, the Indian state can, and will, continue to use substantial force to curb the insurgency, domestic and international criticism notwithstanding.

Sumit Ganguly has suggested that the Government of India can offer significant sop in the immediate and long term, including the return of Kashmir to its pre-1953 status.

General Musharraf's four-point formula, too, had advocated self-governance or autonomy, but not independence. He wanted Kashmir to have soft borders, but people to be allowed to move freely within the region and to implement the road map by the joint efforts of India, Pakistan and Kashmir. Lastly, he suggested the withdrawal of troops in a phased manner. Later, Musharraf said his points were confidence-building and a beginning of the process of resolution of the Kashmir issue.

It is Khurshid Mahmud Kasuri, who, in his book, *Neither a Hawk Nor a Dove*, very candidly admitted, 'Despite many wars that Pakistan and India had fought, it is evident that neither could coerce the other into accepting its position on Kashmir. It should also be clear by now that the two countries had realized the following points; (i) J&K cannot be made independent (ii) borders cannot be redrawn (iii) the Line of Control can and should be made 'irrelevant' and (iv) a joint mechanism for both parts of Kashmir can be worked out.[32]

RESOLUTION, NOT MANAGEMENT, NEED OF THE HOUR

If so much has been discussed, deliberated and diagnosed, it is time we take a pause to evaluate whether any more acts of violence and protest can achieve some of the objectives some sections of the society seem to be chasing. It is time for the common people to draw a balance sheet of what we gained and what we lost, and chase the achievable, realistic, specific and time-bound goals to guide the destiny of our future generations. Children have died, lost their eyesight. Women have been dishonoured and widowed. Men have lost active years of their adult life languishing in prisons. Many killings were bizarre; an old man of 87 years, for example, Maulana Masoodi, religious leader Maulvi Farooq, leading politician Abdul Ghani Lone, educationist Mushir-ul-Haq and many others lost their lives to the battlecry of the national anthem of Jammu and Kashmir National Liberation Front (JKNLF) in the early 1990s and before.

Ek hal, ek umang, guerilla jang, guerilla jang;
Azadi ka ek hi dhang, guerilla jang, guerilla jang

[Our one objective, our one desire, guerilla war, guerilla war;
There is only one way to freedom, guerilla war, guerilla war].

Such killings that defy logic and rationale still continue. Highly acclaimed Shujaat Bhukhari, 50 years of age, editor-in-chief of *Rising Kashmir*, a Srinagar-based newspaper, was shot dead outside his office by unidentified gunmen on 14 June 2018 in the busy Press Enclave area of Lal Chowk, Srinagar.

A lot of blood has already dirtied the water of the Jhelum. Over 1,00,000 people are reported to have lost their lives, either at the hands of militants or security forces, or are simply missing. Over 3,50,000 Kashmiri Pandits have been deprived the opportunity to grow up in a composite culture. It has affected the mental health of people.

Kashmir needs a visionary reformer leader like Zain-ul-Abidin who can provide social, economic and political justice to his people. A Sheikh Abdullah of the early 1940s who can mobilize people for secularism and itehad (unity). A Lal Ded and a Nund Rishi, who can awaken our souls. Monthly congregations at Chrar-e-Sharif Shrine of Nund Rishi can provide occasion for collective mourning and remorse for our leaders and people. At some level, all of us are responsible for the death and tragedy of our people, some for becoming agents of provocateurs, and the rest for remaining silent.

Leaders like Atal Bihari Vajpayee and Pandit Jawaharlal Nehru were statesmen. Both, in their own ways, tried to build public opinion in J&K and the rest of India for deeper understanding and an amicable solution to the problems that plague the state. They have left pearls of wisdom to guide us. Addressing the Lok Sabha on 26 June 1952, Jawaharlal Nehru had said that as opposed to compulsion and coercion, if the people of Kashmir do not want to accede to Pakistan, it will not happen. He further stated that an open mind and heart were the most important factors to contribute to real integration, unlike a consolidation born out of prejudice.

Various Indian leaders have promised a lot to Kashmiris. P.V. Narasimha Rao, then prime minister, on 14 November 1995 addressed the nation from Burkina Faso, a west African nation, and offered to make the land a peer to paradise, Jannat-i-Nishaani. He declared no change in Article 370. Atal Bihari Vajpayee is remembered for his three famous words of wisdom—insaniyat (humanity), jhamooriyat (democracy) and Kashmiriyat (synergic culture)—which intended to seek a resolution.

But even today, integration of the heart and the mind remains an open issue. To approach a solution through Pareto optimal equilibrium in society requires a deep understanding and compassion towards LeLaMOKSHI and dimensions such as country, province, region and identity, if we are to resolve the dispute rather than just manage the situation on the ground from time to time. The genesis of the dispute as one digs deeper in a LeLaMOKSHI framework is not 15 August 1947, one finds, but 16 October 1586 when Srinagar became a cantonment of the Mughals. Since then, the society is meandering to attain its Nash Equilibrium or Pareto optimal equilibrium again. But, above all, Kashmiris of all stock, irrespective of religion, gender, caste, political ideologies and belief systems, need to come together and agree on a common vision of government, enterprise, culture, engagement, education and digital policy for our future generations and habitat. Only then can we have a common list and a unifying slogan.

Chyain kath, myain kath
Sahi kath, akh kath

[Your wish, my wish
Right wish, one wish]

Jahangir loved Kashmir and Kashmiris. He did not find any difference between a Kashmiri Muslim and a Kashmiri Pandit. He wanted to die in Kashmir. I am no Jehangir but if someone were to ask me on my deathbed what my last wish was, perhaps I, too, would say,

Az Ashok damch nazah chu justand
Ba khawahish-i-dil gult ki Kashmir hech

(When Ashok was asked on his deathbed what his last wish was, he replied from his heart: Kashmir, and nothing else).

APPENDIX-1
EXODUS OF KASHMIRI PANDITS

Exodus	Ruler	Remarks
First Exodus 1389–1413	Sikander of the Shah Mir dynasty	Sikander, disdainfully referred to as the 'iconoclast', issued a decree ordering the Pandits to convert to Islam (raliv), opt for exile (tsaliv) or choose to die (galiv). He unleashed mass destruction on Hindu shrines, including the Martand temple. He was helped by Saif-ud-din, a Hindu who had converted recently to Islam. Most Pandits either converted, fled Kashmir or lost their lives. Only eleven Pandit families are reported to have survived this phase of tyranny to stay back in the Valley.
Second Exodus 1506–1585	Chak dynasty	Post the long and peaceful reign of Zain-ul-Abidin (1420–1470), during which most Pandits who had fled earlier returned honourably to the Valley, the Chaks heaped untold misery on them by imposing taxes for practicing religious rites, driving many to seek shelter outside Kashmir.

Exodus	Ruler	Remarks
Third Exodus 1658–1707	Aurangzeb through Iftikar Khan	Mughal subedars appointed by Aurangzeb became tyrants. The goodwill gained by earlier Mughal rulers was eroded. Aurangzeb sent no less than fourteen governors from Delhi during a reign of forty-nine years. During the rule of Iftikar Khan (1671–75), the Pandits approached Guru Tegh Bahadur,[33] the ninth sikh Guru, at Anandpur, and sought his intervention. This led to the guru's martyrdom and conversion of the Sikh community into the fighting Khalsas under his son, Guru Gobind Singh.
Fourth Exodus 1752–1819	Afghans	Sixty-seven years of Afghan rule reduced Kashmir to misery. Kailash Dhar, a leading noble of Kashmir, was beheaded in open court to unleash a reign of fear. Central taxes were also imposed, irrespective of caste, creed and religion.
Fifth Exodus 1931	Hari Singh	A group of young Kashmiri Muslim intellectuals, led by Sheikh Mohammad Abdullah, stoked Muslim resentment over employment of Pandits in government jobs in Kashmir. On 13 July 1931, the Pandits once again became targets of a religious frenzy. Their properties were burnt and some lives were lost. Some victims of sectarian strife left their homes. Dr Nand Lal Zutshi, an eminent Kashmiri Pandit, was one such Pandit whose home was looted in Chinkral Mohalla in Srinagar.

Exodus	Ruler	Remarks
Sixth Exodus 1986	Gul Shah (Chief Minister)	Gul Shah, the brother-in-law of Dr Farooq Abdullah, seized power for twenty months. His brief reign was marked by anarchy, a complete breakdown of administration and, worst of all, communal tensions that threatened to explode into a major upheaval. Shah himself played a diabolical game of inciting the Muslims against the Hindus by raising the slogan of *Islam khatre mein hain* (Islam is in danger). Southern Kashmir was targeted, temples desecrated and properties destroyed. Some Pandits left the comfort of their homes to seek shelter elsewhere.
Seventh Exodus 1990 onwards	Jag Mohan (Governor)	During the month of January 1990, about 1,100 mosques in the entire Valley blared slogans in unison through loudspeakers that generated anxiety, panic and fear among the peace-loving minority Pandit community. Pandits were convinced of their fragile existence, with no guarantee of safety and security after the selective killings of Kashmiri Pandits had reached a crescendo. On 19 January 1990, the continued slogans created a hostile environment for secular, liberal and pro-Indian people in the Valley. Two such slogans were '*Kashir banawon Pakistan, bataw varaie, batneiw saan*'.

Exodus	Ruler	Remarks
		[We will turn Kashmir into Pakistan, along with Kashmiri Pandit women, but without their menfolk.] and *'People's League ka kya paigam, Fateh, Azadi our Islam'*.[What is the message of the People's League? Victory, Freedom and Islam.] Almost the entire population of 3,50,000 Kashmiri Pandits left Kashmir beginning 19 January 1990 and are yet to return to their homes.

ENDNOTES

1 Manoj Joshi, *The Lost Rebellion: Kashmir in the Nineties*, Penguin India, 1999.

2 Stephen Philip Cohen, 'India, Pakistan and Kashmir', in *India as an Emerging Power*, Sumit Ganguly (Ed.), Routledge, 2003.

3 Mudasir Yaqoob, (20 January 2016), 'Gawkadal Massacre Anniversary Today—Survivors Recount Bloodbath', http://www. greaterkashmir.com/news/srinagarcity/story/207443.html

4 Manoj Joshi, *The Lost Rebellion: Kashmir in the Nineties*, Penguin India, 1999.

5 B.K. Bakshi, *Kashmir Kidnapping*, Dr P.N. Singh Centre for HRD, Mumbai, 2012.

6 B.K. Bakshi, *Kashmir Kidnapping*, Dr P.N. Singh Centre for HRD, Mumbai, Preface, v, 2012.

7 P.N.K. Bamzai, *A History of Kashmir: Political-Social-Cultural*, Srinagar: Gulshan Books, p 455, 2008.

8 P.N.K. Bamzai, *A History of Kashmir: Political-Social-Cultural*,

Gulshan Books, p 457, 2008.

9   Jawahar Lal Bhat, 'Lal-Ded Revisited', Vision Creative Services, 2015.

10 Kushanava Choudhary, (November 2000), 'After the Lahore Summit: The Real Story', rediff.com, http://www.rediff.com/news/2000/nov.23naik.htm.

11 Khurshid Mahmud Kasuri, *Neither a Hawk Nor a Dove: An Insider's Account of Pakistan's Foreign Policy*, Viking Press, Penguin Books India, 2015.

12 Vinay Kaura, *Countering Insurgency in Kashmir: The Cyber Dimension*, ORF Occasional Paper No. 106, January 2017.

13 Praveen Swami, 'A War to End War: The Causes and Outcomes of the 2001-2002 India-Pakistan Crisis' in *Nuclear Proliferation in South Asia Crisis Behaviour and the Bomb*, Sumit Ganguly and S. Paul Kapur (eds.), Routledge, 2008.

14 P.N.K. Bamzai, *A History of Kashmir: Political-Social-Cultural*, Srinagar: Gulshan Books, p 479, 2008.

15 Jean Drèze and Amartya Sen, *An Uncertain Glory*, Allen Lane, 2013.

16 D.D. Thakur, *My Life and Years in Kashmir Politics*, Konark Publishers, pp. 351-353, 2005.

17 'Regional Energy Cooperation: Accessing and Developing Hydrocarbon Resources in South Asia', *ORF Seminar Series*, Vol. 1, Issue 11, May 2013.

18 S.A. Bhat and N. Imtiaz, 'Drug Addiction in Kashmir: Issues and Challenges', *Journal of Drug Abuse*, Vol. 3 No. 19, September 22, 2017, http://drugabuse.imedpub.com/

19 Ibid.

20 Alastair Lamb, *Crisis in Kashmir: 1947-1966*, Routledge, 1966.

21 Christopher Snedden, *Kashmir: The Unwritten History*, HarperCollins, 2013.

22 Letter by Lord Mountbatten to Maharaja Hari Singh, 27 October 1947.

23 Prem Shankar Jha, *Kashmir 1947: Rival Versions of History*, Oxford India, Appendix III, p 143, 1996.

24 Elie Kedourie, *Nationalism*, Hutchison, 1960.

25 Adeed Dawisha, *Nation and Nationalism: Historical Antecedents to Contemporary Debates*, International Studies Association, Blackwill Publishing, 2002.

26 Ellie Kedourie, *Nationalism*, Hutchison, 1960.

27 A.G. Noorani, *The Kashmir Dispute: 1947-2012*. Vol. 2. New Delhi, Tulika Books, 2013.

28 Surapati Pramanik and Tapan Kumar Roy, 'Game Theoretic Model to the Jammu and Kashmir Conflict between India and Pakistan', *International Journal of Mathematical Archive*, pp. 162-170, 2013.

29 S.A. Rid, 'Kashmir: The Prisoner's Dilemma for India and Pakistan, Peace Prints', *South Asian Journal of Peacekeeping*, Vol. 4, No. 2, Winter, 2012.

30 The Future of Kashmir, BBC News Online, http://www.news.bbc.co.uk

31 Devesh Khandelwal, *Pledge for an Integrated India*, Prabhat Prakashan, p 60, 2015.

32 Khurshid Mahmud Kasuri, *Neither a Hawk Nor a Dove: An Insider's Account of Pakistan's Foreign Policy*, Penguin Books India, 2015.

33 P.N.K. Bamzai, *A History of Kashmir: Political-Social-Cultural*, Srinagar: Gulshan Books, p 401, 2008.

EPILOGUE

My beloved karmayogi father, friend, philosopher and guide, Soom Nath Dhar, breathed his last at the residence of my younger brother, Ravinder, in Jammu on the night of 1 January 2018. Through happiness and sadness, he lived by the values of a synergic culture till he left his physical body.

After the internal displacement of Kashmiri Pandits from the Valley to distant parts of India and abroad, it has become a practice to place obituary messages in the *Daily Excelsior*, a newspaper in Jammu, and *Greater Kashmir* in Srinagar, to inform near and dear ones. So did we.

I recall my father receiving a telephone call from one of his cousins in Jammu when he was staying with us in Kolkata in March 2016.

The caller said, 'I have not been able to reach you. Your landline in Jammu was not working. I got your Kolkata number today. Hope you are well.'

'Don't you read *Daily Excelsior* and *Greater Kashmir*?' my father asked.

'Yes, I do,' replied his cousin.

'Have you seen my photo on the obituary page? If you have not, then you should assume that I am alive and kicking, and am either with my daughter, Sarla, in Gurgaon, or with my son, Ashok, in Kolkata,' Papa replied.

The obituary in these newspapers, I realized, was indeed read by family members, friends and well-wishers in Srinagar and Jammu. It was an overwhelming feeling to see our friends travelling from Srinagar and other distant places to be with us at the crematorium at Shastri Nagar, Jammu, on 2 January 2018. Kalpana, my wife, and I reached in time from Kolkata to perform the final rites and related rituals.

My friends, Sarwar Dar, Amrit Pal Singh, Kursheed Ganai and many others stood by my side at the crematorium. The Chandrabhaga Community Hall, Canal Road, Jammu had Muslims, Sikhs, Kashmiri Pandits and Dogras gathered to attend the prayer meeting to celebrate his eventful and long life. Amidst the chanting of vedic mantras and kirtans by the devotees of ISKCON, Jammu, it became abundantly clear to me that it is a daunting task for our adversaries to destroy the synergic roots of our state.

On arrival from Kolkata, when I offered Gangajal to my father, Sarwar stood by my side silently, wishing to do likewise. Sarla asked him to go ahead and feel free to offer Gangajal to my father. He respectfully did so. My father had been as affectionate to him as his father to me. Kashmiriyat may be dormant, but surely it is not dead.

Three days before he passed away, my father had asked Ravi to start his car to take him to our home in Jawahar Nagar, Srinagar. It was perhaps his last wish to die in the house he had built with his sweat and struggle, but he had not been in a condition fit to travel.

In the last week of June, last year, Kalpana and I performed *pind daan*, a ritual for departed souls, for my parents in

Badrinath, Uttarakhand. The next day, early in the morning, I saw my father in a dream. He was dressed in a grey pheran, a Kashmiri gown, with a black kurakuli (special fur) cap, holding a cigarette between his little finger and ring finger, standing on the verandah of our house in Jawahar Nagar. 'Papa, you here?' I asked.

'Well, Ravi did not bring me here. This house is not being looked after well, and I see it is vacant, unsafe. Good, I am here now.' I looked inside and surprisingly found no one in the two-storey house. He looked at me and said, 'You too miss being here. Come and join me.'

I hope and pray for the beginning of a new dawn in Kashmir when we feel safe enough to return home and not wait for departed souls to make the Valley secure for us.

ACKNOWLEDGEMENTS

I thank my late mother, Sheila Dhar, my father, Soom Nath Dhar, and my family for passing on the spirit of Kashmiriyat to me, a dominant theme in this book. I would have been unable to write this book had Professor Rakhahari Chatterji, former Dean of Arts, University of Calcutta, not given me the confidence and encouragement to do so. Post relocation to Kolkata in April 2015, I started writing and tested his patience many a time, with various draft chapters. Thanks a ton, Rakhaharida, for bearing with a non-scholar and being a pillar of support to me.

I am especially indebted to Dr Manoj Joshi, author of two books on Kashmir, *Lost Rebellion* and *Untold Story*, and Sunjoy Joshi, Chairman, Observer Research Foundation (ORF). Dr Joshi not only suggested reference books from time to time for me to read but also reviewed the manuscript and agreed to write the 'Foreword'. Sunjoy encouraged me and critically reviewed the draft and made valuable suggestions for structuring the narrative. My sincere and grateful thanks to my colleagues from Kumaon, my second home.

I was very fortunate and blessed to get the draft manuscript reviewed and commented upon by many experts with diverse backgrounds. I am grateful to Krishnan Srinivasan, former

Indian foreign secretary; Professor Sumit Ganguly, author of *Crisis in Kashmir* and professor at Indiana University, the US; Professor Hari Vasudevan, Department of History, University of Calcutta; Professor Jayanta Bandyopadhyaya, IIM Calcutta and IISc, Bangalore; Professor Bandana Chatterjee, sociologist; and T.K. Arun, Senior Editor (Opinion), *The Economic Times*. Girish Shirodkar, Partner, Strategy, a part of PricewaterhouseCoopers; and Dr Nilanjan Ghosh, economist, Director, 2009, ORF, reviewed the last chapter, especially the use of strategic planning tools for conflict resolution. Many thanks to them.

During the course of my research, I met many persons whose words of encouragement and inputs have been of immense help. Thanks to Ratan Watal, former Indian finance secretary; Colonel O.P. Bhatia (rtd.); Lieutenant General Vinod Bhatia (rtd.); Brigadier Deepak Sinha (rtd.); Dr Manzoor Sayyed Qazi; Anil Dhar, former IRS officer; college friends Farooq Wani, Sarwar Dar and Amrit Pal Singh; Rosy Kaul, budding banker and blogger; Renuka Mishra, Trustee, ORF; Professor R.K. Ogra; Upinder Jalali, senior advocate; and groups of Kashmiri youth with diverse background, who I met in Srinagar during my visits in 2017. Thanks also to Pratnashree Basu, Ambalika Guha and my Facebook friends for their help.

It has been an enriching experience to read the scholarly works of so many authors as listed in the bibliography and mentioned in the book. Thanks to all authors whose work has been cited and acknowledged. Thanks also to the staff of the National Library, Alipore, Kolkata; the Asiatic Society Library, Kolkata; and J&K state archives, Jammu, for allowing me access to relevant publications and books.

The draft manuscript was typed out by Geetha S. Kumar and copy edited by Dr Rita Banerjee. I appreciate their painstaking efforts to put it in a format that interested publishers. Yamini Chowdhury, Senior Commissioning Editor, Priya Talwar, Assistant Commissioning Editor, and Anukta Ghosh, Copy Editor, Rupa Publications, and the rest of the team at Rupa helped refine the book and bring it to its current shape. My grateful thanks to them. A special note of thanks to Kapish G. Mehra, Managing Director, Rupa Publications, New Delhi, for publishing the work of a new author and adding me to the august list of authors at the prestigious Rupa family.

Lastly, words are not enough to acknowledge the silent and steadfast support of my educationist wife, Kalpana. She has been a great source of encouragement throughout our married life. I truly hope our progeny, Rohit and Siddharth, now settled in the US, will assimilate the richness of our culture and keep the flag of Kashmiriyat and lihaaz flying high wherever they live, and pass on their learnings to the next generation.

BIBLIOGRAPHY/REFERENCES

BOOKS

Abdullah, Sheikh Mohammad. *The Blazing Chinar*. Srinagar: Gulshan Books, 2013.

Akbar, M.J. *Kashmir: Behind the Vale*. New Delhi: Penguin, 1991.

Akbar, M.J. *Tinderbox: The Past and Future of Pakistan*. New Delhi: HarperCollins, 2011.

Akbar, M.J. *India: The Seige Within*. Suffolk: Penguin, 1985.

Arberry, J. *An Introduction to the History of Sufism*. Islamic Book Trust, October 2015.

Bakhshi, B.K. *Kashmir Kidnapping*. Mumbai: Work Centre Offset Printers, 2012.

Bamzai, P.N.K. *A History of Kashmir*. Srinagar: Gulshan Books, 2008.

Bamzai, P.N.K. *Socio-Economic History of Kashmir 1846-1925*. Srinagar: Gulshan Books, 2007.

Basu, Arabinda and Anadi Pal. *Human Remains from Burzahom*. Anthropological Survey of India, Govt. of India, March 1980.

Bhat, Jawahar Lal. *Lal-Ded Revisited*. Vision Creative Services, 2014.

Bhat, R.L. *Intikhaabi Taarikhi Kashmir*. Kashmir: Gulshan Books, 2016.

Borkakoti, J. *International Trade: Causes and Consequences—An Empirical and Theoretical Text*. Springer, 1998.

Claridge, Duane R. *A Spy for All Seasons: My Life in the CIA*. New York: Scribner, 1997.

Cohen, Stephen Philip. 'India, Pakistan and Kashmir', *India as an*

Emerging Power. Sumit Ganguly (Ed.). Routledge, 2003.

Das Gupta, Jyoti Bhusan. *Jammu and Kashmir.* The Hague: Martinus Nijhoff, 1968.

Dasgupta, C. *War and Diplomacy in Kashmir.* 1947–48, Sage, 2002.

Daulat, A.S. and Aditya Sinha. *Kashmir: The Vajpayee Years.* New Delhi: HarperCollins, 2015.

Dhar, P.N. *Indira Gandhi: The Emergency and Indian Democracy.* Oxford University Press, 2000.

Dreze, Jean and Amartya Sen. *An Uncertain Glory: India and its Contradictions.* London: Allen Lane, Penguin Books, 2013.

Fazili, Manzoor Ahmad. *Kashmir Predilection.* Srinagar: Gulshan Publishers, 1988.

Ganguly, Sumit. *The Crisis in Kashmir: Portents of War, Hopes of Peace.* Woodrow Wilson Center Press and Cambridge University Press, USA, 1998.

Gorman, Michael E. *Transforming Nature: Ethics, Invention and Discovery.*Springer, 1998.

Hanif, N. *Biographical Encyclopaedia of Sufis (South Asia).* Sarup & Sons, 2000.

Hassanain, Fida Mohammad Khan. *Historic Kashmir.* Srinagar: Gulshan Books, 2012.

Haqqani, Hussain. *Reimagining Pakistan: Transforming a Dysfunctional Nuclear State.* India: HarperCollins, 2018.

Jagmohan. *My Frozen Turbulence in Kashmir.* Allied Publishers, May 1991.

Jalali, Girdhari Lal. *Untold Jihad in Kashmir: A Critical Analysis.* New Delhi: Vakil Publications, 2010.

Joshi, Manoj. *Kashmir 1947–1965: A Story Retold.* New Delhi: India Research Press, 2008.

Joshi, Manoj. *The Lost Rebellion: Kashmir in the Nineties.* Penguin Books India, 1999.

Kak, Subhash. Jammu and Kashmir, World Encyclopaedia, Oxford University Press, 2005.

Kalhana. *Rajtarangini: A Chronicle of the Kings of Kashmir.* Vols. 1, 2 and 3. Srinagar: Gulshan Books, 2007.

Kasuri, Khurshid Mahmud. *Neither a Hawk Nor a Dove: An Insider's Account of Pakistan's Foreign Policy.* Penguin Books India, 2015.

Kaul, J.L. *Kashmiri Lyrics.* Srinagar: Rinemisray, 1945.

Kedourie, Elie. *Nationalism.* Hutchison, 1960.

Khan, Nyla Ali. *Islam, Women, and Violence in Kashmir: Between India and Pakistan.* Springer, 2010.

Khandelwal, Devesh. *Pledge for an Integrated India.* New Delhi: Prabhat Prakashan, 2015.

Knight, Edward Frederick. *Kashmir and Tibet.* New Delhi: Mittal Publications, 1984.

Kothiara, Verghese. *Crafting Peace in Kashmir: Through A Realist Lens.* Sage Publications, 2004.

Lawrence, Walter R. *The Valley of Kashmir.* Srinagar: Gulshan Books, 2011.

Maheshwari, Anil. *Crescent over Kashmir: Politics of Mullaism.* South Asia Books, September 1993.

Menon, V.P. *The Story of the Integration of the Indian States.* Longmans, Green & Co., 1955.

Naipaul, V.S. *An Area of Darkness: His Discovery of India*, Picador, 2010.

Nehru, Jawaharlal. Jawahar Lal Nehru's Speeches. Vol. 2. Ministry of Information and Broadcasting, Government of India, January 1954.

Noorani, A.G. *The Kashmir Dispute 1947–2012.* Vol. 2. New Delhi: Tulika Books, 2013.

Pal, Pratapaditya. *The Arts of Kashmir.* New York: Asia Society and Five Continents, USA, 2008.

Pandita, Rahul. *Our Moon has Blood Clots: The Exodus of Kashmiri Pandits.* Random House India, 2013.

Parashar, Pramanand. *Kashmir and the Freedom Movement.* New Delhi: Sarup & Sons, 2004.

Peer, Basharat. *Curfewed Night.* Random House India, 2009.

Quraishi, Humra. *Kashmir: The Untold Story.* New Delhi: Penguin, 2004.

Raina, Piya Ray (Saddhak). *Socio-cultural and Religious Traditions of Kashmiri Pandits.* Georgia: Nee Roh Inc., 2006.

Rivera, Julio César. 'The Scope and Structure of Civil Codes—Relations with Commercial Law, Family Law, Consumer Law and Private International Law: A Comparative Approach' in *The Scope and Structure of Civil Codes*. Springer, December 2013.

Rizvi, Saiyid Athar Abbas. *A History of Sufism in India*. Munshiram Manoharlal Publishers, 1994.

Sehegal, Narendra. *Converted Kashmir: A Bitter Saga of Religious Conversion*. Utpal Publications, 1994.

Shauq, Shafi. *Lalla Dyad: The Mystic Kashmiri Poetess*. Srinagar: Gulshan Books, 2015.

Singh, Balbir. *State Politics in India: Explorations in Political Processes in Jammu and Kashmir*. New Delhi: Macmillan India, 1982.

Singh, Karan. *Autobiography*. New Delhi: Oxford University Press, 1989.

Snedden, Christopher. *Kashmir: The Unwritten History*. New Delhi: HarperCollins, India, 2013.

Snedden, Christopher. *Understanding Kashmir and Kashmiris*. London: Hurst & Company, 2015.

Swami, Praveen. 'A War to End War: The Causes and Outcomes of the 2001–2002 India-Pakistan Crisis' in *Nuclear Proliferation in South Asia Crisis Behaviour and the Bomb*, Sumit Ganguly and S. Paul Kapur (eds.). Routledge, 2008.

The Statesman's Yearbook: The Politics, Cultures and Economies of the World 2017. Palgrave Macmillan, 2016.

Wakhlu, Somnath. *Hari Singh: The Maharaja, the Man, the Times*. National Publishing House, January 2006.

Wakhlu, Somnath. *The Rich Heritage of Jammu and Kashmir: Studies in Art, Architecture, History and Culture of the Region*. New Delhi: Gyan Publishing House, 1998.

Wani, Feroz Ahmad. *The Politics of State Autonomy in Jammu and Kashmir*. Srinagar: Book Palace, 2015.

Wani, G.A. *Kashmir History and Politics 1846–1983*. Srinagar: G.A. Wani, 1986.

Wani, Gull Mohammad. 'Political Assertion of Kashmiri Identity' in *The*

Parchment of Kashmir, Nyla Ali Khan (ed.). Palgrave Macmillan, August 2012.

Zikamabahari, J.D.D. *The Attainment of Self-determination in African States by Rebels.* Northwest University, December 2014.

Zutshi, Chitralekha. *Languages of Belonging: Islam, Regional Identity and the Making of Kashmir.* Permanent Black, 2003.

ARTICLES & MAGAZINES

Abdullah, Sheikh Mohammad. 'Kashmir, India and Pakistan', *Foreign Affairs*, April 1965, https://www.foreignaffairs.com/articles/asia/1965-04-01/kashmir-india-and-pakistan

Alam, Afroz. 'Towards Solving Kashmir Imbroglio', *The Statesman*, Kolkata, 19 August, 2017.

Bala, Madhu. 'Economic Policy and State Owned Enterprises: Evolution Towards Privatisation in India', *MPRA Paper* No. 17946, October 2009.

Baloch, N.A. and A.Q. Rafiqi. 'The Regions of Sind, Baluchistan, Multan and Kashmir: The Historical, Social and Economic Setting', UNESCO.

Bamzai, Sandeep. 'America's Great Fishing Expedition in Kashmir', *ORF Special Report* No. 23, August 2016.

Bhatt, S. 'The Nature and Consciousness of the People of Kashmir', *Himalayan Central Asian Studies*, Vol. 1, No. 3, Oct–Dec 1997.

Bonikowski, Bart. 'Nationalism in Settled Times', *Annual Review of Sociology*, Vol. 42, July 2016.

Bradnock, Robert W. 'Kashmir: Paths to Peace', *Chatham House*, May 2010.

Chakravartty, Nikhil. 'Kashmir: Setting the Priorities', *Mainstream Weekly*, Vol. LIII, No 13, 21 March 2015.

Choudhury, Kushanava. 'After the Lahore Summit: The Real Story', *The Rediff Special*, rediff.com.

Coase, Ronald H. 'Blackmail', Occasional Paper No. 24, University of Chicago Law School, 1998.

Dar, Fayaz Ahmad. 'Living in a Pressure Cooker Situation: A Needs

Assessment of Youth in India-administered Kashmir', *Conciliation Resources*, August 2011.

Dawisha, Adeed. 'Nation and Nationalism: Historical Antecedents to Contemporary Debates', *International Studies Review*, Vol. 4, No. 1, Spring 2002.

Drompp, Michael R. 'Breaking the Orkhon Tradition: Kirghiz Adherence to the Yensei Region after AD 840', *Journal of the American Oriental Society*, Vol. 119, No. 3, July–September, 1999.

Evans, Alexander. 'A Departure from History: Kashmiri Pandits, 1990–2001', *Contemporary South Asia*, Vol. 11, Issue 1, Taylor & Francis, 2002.

Evans, Alexander. 'The Kashmir Insurgency: As Bad as it Gets', *Small Wars and Insurgencies*, Vol. 11, Issue 1, Taylor & Francis, 2000.

Fearon, James D. 'Separatist Wars, Partition, and World Order', *Journal of Security Studies*, Taylor & Francis, 25 January 2007.

Fresacher, Sonja. 'How Does the Perceived Terrorism Risk Influence the Travel Decision to Jammu and Kashmir', Modul University, Vienna, June 2012.

Halder, Debarati and K. Jaishankar. 'Property Rights of Hindu Women: A Feminist Review of Succession Laws of Ancient, Medieval, and Modern India', *Journal of Law and Religion*, Vol. 24, Issue 2, 24 April 2015.

Hardgrave Jr. Robert L. Peter John Brobst, Mstapha Kamal Pasha, Sumit Ganguly, and Premshankar Jha. 'Kashmir 1947: Burdens of the Past, Options for the Future: Four Perspectives', *Commonwealth & Comparative Politics*, Vol. 36, Issue 1, Taylor & Francis, March 1998.

'Indira-Sheikh accord a milestone event: Vohra', *Business Standard*, 27 October 2013.

'Jammu and Kashmir Interlocutors' Report', Bharatiya Janata Party, August 2012.

Kachroo, Janki Nath. 'From the Pages of History', *Milchar*, Mumbai, India, 2011.

Kak, Subhash. 'The Poplar and the China: Kashmir in a Historical Outline', *International Journal of Indian Studies*, Vol. 3, 1993.

Kaul, T.N. 'What is at Stake in Kashmir?', *Koshur Samachar*, Kashmiri Samiti, Delhi, Oct-Nov 1992.

Kumar, Sumita. 'Pakistan's Strategic Thinking', *Strategic Analysis*, Vol. 35, Issue 3, Taylor & Francis, 2011.

Mathur, Shubh. 'Memory and Hope: New Perspectives on the Kashmir Conflict: An Introduction', *The Sociological Review*, Vol. 56, Issue 2, Sage, 29 September 2014.

Milchar, published by the Kashmiri Pandits Association, Mumbai.

Mishra, Satish. 'Need to Grab Initiative on J&K: Working Group Reports' Recommendations Require a Push', *ORF Commentary*, New Delhi.

Mukherjee, Anit. 'A Brand New Day or Back to the Future? The Dynamics of India-Pakistan Relations', *India Review*, Vol. 8, No. 4, Routledge, December 2009.

Naad, published by the All India Kashmiri Samaj

Narayan, Jayaprakash. Letter: 'Then, as Now', Jayaprakash Narayan, *Greater Kashmir*, Srinagar, 4 September 2016.

Nayar, Kuldip. 'Kashmir: Re-reading its Past in Order to Proffer a Practicable Solution', *The Round Table*, Vol. 81, Issue 323, Taylor & Francis, 1992.

Noorani, A.G. 'How to Settle the Kashmir Issue', *Frontline*, 16 October, 2015.

Pandita, K.N. 'Kashmir Question', *Kashmir Herald*, February 2003.

Pramanik, S and Roy, T.K. Game Theoretic Model to the Jammu and Kashmir Conflict between India and Pakistan, *International Journal of Mathematical Archive*, 2013, pp 162-170.

Pubby, Manu. 'Abdullah Knew of Pakistan's Design in 60s, CIA Didn't Believe it: Agent-turned-private Spy', *The Indian Express*, 26 January 2011.

Rid, S.A. 'Kashmir: The Prisoner's Dilemma for India and Pakistan, 'Peace Prints', *South Asian Journal of Peacekeeping*, Vol. 4, No. 2 Winter, 2012.

Singh, Khushwant. 'Iqbal's Hindu Relations', *The Telegraph*, Calcutta, 30 June 2007.

Thomas, Raju, G.C., 'Secessionist Movements in South Asia', *Survival*, Vol. 36, Issue 2, Taylor & Francis, 1994.

Tikoo, Tej Kumar. 'Kashmiri Pandits Offered Three Choices by Radical Islamists', *Indian Defence Review*, 19 January 2015.

Tremblay, Reeta Chowdhari. 'Kashmir: The Valley's Political Dynamics', *Contemporary South Asia*, Vol. 4, Issue 1, Taylor & Francis, 1995.

Trisal, O.N. 'Islamic Fundamentalism in Kashmir', *Political History of Kashmir*, April 2017.

Vitasta, published by the Kashmir Sabha, Kolkata.

Whitehead, Andrew. 'Kashmir's Conflicting Identities', *History*, Workshop Journal, Vol. 58, Issue 1, 2004.

NEWSPAPERS

Bokhari, Syed Sharif Hussain. 'Kashmir: Accession Saga and Aftermath', *Pakistan Observer*.

'Initiatives on Kashmir Should be Taken Forward: Chidambaram', *The Pioneer*, 2 October 2013.

Nayar, Kuldip. 'Why Kashmir remains disturbed', *The Daily Star*, 16 May 2016.

Nayar, Kuldip. 'A Visit to Srinagar', *The Statesman*, Kolkata, 12 May 2016.

Singh, Khushwant, 'Iqbal's Hindu Relations', *The Telegraph*, 30 June 2007.

Zafar, Mustafa. 'When Iqbal called for a Muslim India, within India', *Dawn*, 18 November 2015.

The Times of India, 6 September 2004.

The Times of India, 10 November 2001.

The Times of India, 11 July 2000

The Times of India, 1995 (April 4 and 5; September 20; November 16)

The Times of India, 14 January 1994

The Times of India, 3 August 1990

The Times of India, 16 September 1983

The Times of India, 14 October 1975

The Times of India, 1972 (January 6; February 3, 13, and 29; March 3 and 16; May 7 and 18; July 4, 13, 19 and 29; August 11, 13 and

30; October 1)

The Times of India, 29 December 1966.

The Times of India, 1965 (August 13, 24 and 25;October 13)

The Times of India, 1964 (April 25 and 29; May 12; July 5 and 17; October 31)

The Times of India, 16 April 1957

The Times of India, 1947-1948

ONLINE REFERENCES:

Allana, G. *Pakistan Movement Historical Documents*. Karachi: Department of International Relations University of Karachi, 1969, pp. 103–110, http://bit.ly/2dOH9ng

Bhat, SA and Imtiaz N. *Drug Addiction in Kashmir: Issues and Challenges*. Journal of Drug Abuse, Vol. 3 No. 3:19, 22 September 2017, http://drugabuse.imedpub.com/

'Implications of Article 370', *Facts about Kashmir*, 26 December 2008, http://facts-about-kashmir.blogspot.in/

'Jammu and Kashmir', *Encyclopaedia of India*, 2006,http://www.encyclopedia.com/international/encyclopedias-almanacs-transcripts-and-maps/jammu-and-kashmir

'Sainik School Ghorakhal', Uttaranchal, http://www.euttaranchal.com/schools/sainik-school-ghorakhal

'The Era of Kanishka', *A Rough Guide to Kushan History*, http://www.kushan.org/essays/chronology/kanishka.htm

'The Pāratas & King Yolamira (125 AD)', *Shams-i-bala and the Historical Shambhala Kingdom*, 29 July 2015, http://balkhandshambhala.blogspot.in/2015_07_01_archive.html

'The Sick-ular Indoctrination of Indian Children—Part II', *Desi Contrarian*, 2 April 2016, http://www.desicontrarian.com/category/books/

David Steinberg. 'Indian Constitutional Round Table Conferences London 1931-1933', *House of David*, http://www.houseofdavid.ca/round_tab.htm

Lavakare, Arvind. 'J&K Accession Quicksand—A Commentary',

cifjkindia, February 2001, http://www.cifjkindia.org/arvlav/arvlav_030.shtml

Razdan, Vinayak. 'Lyrics, 'yatulikhanjar', *Search Kashmir,* April 23, 2011, http://www.searchkashmir.org/2011/04/lyrics-ya-tuli-khanjar.html

Razdan, Vinayak. 'You know you are a Kashmiri if...', *Search Kashmir,* 6 June 2009, http://www.searchkashmir.org/2009/06/you-know-you-are-kashmiri-if.html

Sharma, Shatakshi. 'Constitutional Integration of Jammu and Kashmir', *Lawctopus,* September 2014, https://www.lawctopus.com/academike/constitutional-intergration-jammu-kashmir/

Shivani Raina-Dhar, 'A Collection of Kashmiri Music, Bhajans and Prayers', *Kashmir Overseas Association,* 22 September 2003

Yaqoob, Mudasir. 'Gawkadal Massacre Anniversary Today: Survivors Recount Bloodbath', 20 January 2016, http://www.greaterkashmir.com/news/srinagarcity/story/207443.html

INDEX

Abdullah, Farooq, 46, 53–54, 126, 130, 132, 163, 203

Abdullah, Sheikh, 35, 41, 43, 46, 49–54, 90, 98, 100–108, 111–113, 115, 119, 120, 125, 138, 163, 167–168, 171, 180, 197.
  1952 agreement, 102
  aligning policy with Indian state, 98
  call for unity, 138
  dismissal and arrest, 105
  'friends' of, 50–55
  lessons from, 111–113
  political influence of, 117
  withdrawal plebiscite demand, 120

Abhinavagupta. *See* Kashmiri Shavism

Accord of 1975, 92, 102–111

Achabal, 23

Adi Shankaracharya, 6

Advaita Vedanta, 19

Afghan rule, 139–143
  cruelties of, 24
  governance model, 81

Afzal Beg, Mirza, 50, 107, 111–112, 120

Ahmed Rid, Saeed, 186

Ahmed, Aziz, 114–116

Aiyar, Mani Shankar, 90, 164

Ajmer Sharif, private visit to, 78

Akbar, 5, 22–23, 26, 41, 133

Al-Baro, 125

Al-Dabbagh Group, 70

Al-Fatah, 125, 154

Ali, Choudhary Rahmat, 38

Al-Kashmir, 125

All India Anna Dravida Munnetra Kazhagam (AIADMK), 108

All India Federation, idea of an, 96

Al-Qaeda, 135

Amarnath, 29

American Civil War, 87

Amin, Mohammad, 163

Aminuddin, Usman, 90

Amritsar Treaty (1846), 24–25

Anand, Mulk Raj, 97

Anglo–Russian plans, 95

Anglo–Russian rivalry, 24, 94

Anglo–Russian strategy, 25

An Area of Darkness, 29

Armed Forces Special Power Act (AFSPA), 156

Arthur, C.W.A., 94

Article 370 (Indian Constitution), 103, 106–107, 113, 189–92, 196

Asian–African Conference, 51

Autobiography, 58, 96

Autonomy, preservation of, 113

Avantivarman (AD 855–883), 19

Awam, Ghazzanfar, 75

Ayyangar, N. Gopalaswami, 107, 120

Azad Kashmir (free Kashmir), 51, 105, 147, 148, 168, 170, 188, 189
Azad Kashmir Radio, 147
Azad, Maulana Abul Kalam, 107
Azam Khan, Mohammad, 24
Aziz, Tariq, 146

Backchannel negotiations, 144–46
Baig, Muzaffar Hussain, 154
Bajaj, Rajeev, 163
Bakshi, B.K., 135
Bamzai, P.N.K., 17
Bandhu, Kashyap, 134
Bangladesh Liberation War (1971), 107, 127, 155
Bangladesh, creation of, 41, 106
BBC News Online solutions, 188–90
    Chenab Formula, 189
    independent Kashmir valley, 189
    independent Kashmir, 188
    independent smaller Kashmir, 189
    Kashmir joins India, 188
    Kashmir joins Pakistan, 188–89
    status quo, 189–90
Beaumont, Christopher, 99, 174
Beg, Afzal, 50, 107, 111–12, 120
Bhan, Pushkar Nath, 147
Bhan, Shereen, 33
Bharatiya Jana Sangh, 103
Bhat, S.A., 164
Bhat, Sabzar, 154
Bhukhari, Shujaat, 197
Bhutto, Benazir, 77–78
Bhutto, Zulfikar Ali, 114–15
Birla, Kumar Mangalam, 163
Black Day, 106
The Blazing Chinar, 41
Bogra, Mohammad Ali, 104, 114
Boundary Commission, 173
British Commonwealth of Nations, 97
Bud Shah. See Zain-ul-Abidin
Buddhism, x, 5–6, 18–19, 178
Buddhist Council, Fourth, 6, 18

Chak, Yousuf Shah, 22–23
Chicago Tribune, 44
Child marriage, 99
China–Pakistan Economic Corridor (CPEC), 163
Choudhury, Kushanava, 145
Chrar-e-Sharif Shrine. See Nund Rishi
CIA, 49, 52–53
Civil war, 87–88
Clarridge, Duane R., 52–53
Cohen, Stephen Philip, 127–28
Collateral damage, 136
Common legacy, 39–42
Conflict resolution, 170, 180, 185, 211
Congress of Vienna, 86
Constructivism, 186
Council of Regency of the British, 94
Counter–insurgency operation, 195
Crafting Peace in Kashmir, 73
The Crisis in Kashmir: Portents of War, Hopes of Peace 195
Crisis in Kashmir: 1947–1966, 166
Cultural amalgamation, 3
Curfewed Nights, 58

Daily Excelsior, 207
Damaras, 26
Dar, Bishan Narayan, 110–11
Dar, Hilal, 153
Dar, Sarwar, 40, 44, 208, 211
Dara Sikoh, 23
Dasgupta, C., 56
Dasgupta, Jyoti Bhusan, 56
Dastgeer Sahib, 12
Death of a Hero, 97
Delhi Agreement (1952), 103
Dhar, Birbal, 24, 139–40
Dhar, D.P., 50, 53, 114–119, 134
Dhar, P.N., 115
Dhar, Sheila, 9
Dhar, Soom Nath, 207
Diwan Chand, Misr, 140
Dixit, J.N., 146

Dixon Plan, 104–05, 145
Dogras, 5, 24–27, 93, 126, 208
Doraiswamy, K., 135
Dove–Hawk game, 186–87
Dramatic 'independence' ceremony, 134
Dravida Munnetra Kazhagam (DMK), 108
Drèze, Jean, 159
Drug menace, 165
Dulat, A.S., 28, 54

Economics vs. emotions, 159–65
E-governance, 162
Enlai, Zhou, 51
Ethno–nationalism, 176

Fard, Ghanimi, 89–90
Faso, Burkina, 196
Fayaz, Ummer, 67
First World War, 94, 182
Fotedar, Shiv Narayan, 134
Fotedar, Vinay, 88

Game theory, 185–86
Ganai, Khurshid Ahmed, 68, 208
Gandhi, Indira, 92, 106–08, 110, 114–19
Gandhi, Mahatma, 99, 153
Gandhi, Rahul, 162
Gandhi, Rajiv, 78
Ganesha temple, 10
Ganguly, Sumit, 83, 195–96, 211
Ganjoo, N.K., 132
Ganpatyar School, 11, 67
Gawkadal massacre, 131–34
Geelani, Syed Ali Shah, 154
Gellner, Ernest, 175
Ghulam Mohammad, Bakshi, 43, 46, 48–53, 105, 115
Gini coefficient, 161
Global Dispute Resolution Models, 181–84
    Aaland model, 182
    Aceh Accord, 184
    Irish model, 183
    Quebec model, 183

South Tyrol model, 182
Trieste–Saar model, 181
Gorkhaland, 69
Graduate Volunteer Service Overseas (GVSO), 67
Greater Kashmir, 149, 207
Guerilla war, 197
Guest control, 149
Gul, Hamid, General, 79
Gul, Mast, 135
Gulab Singh, 24–25, 92, 140
Gymkhana, 72, 75

Haider, Mirza, 22
Haksar, Kailash Nath, 96
Haksar, P.N., 115–16
Haqqani, Husain, 14, 57
Hari Prabhat fort, 23
Hari Singh, 57, 92–102, 106, 132, 167, 171, 179, 188, 202
    doctrine of lapse, 95
    feudal ambition in, 96
    indecisiveness of, 97
    love for horse racing, 98
    mistrust of the British, 96–98
    'misunderstood maharaja', 100
    personal life, 95
    scales of accession, 99–100
    virtual agnostic, 96
Hazelhurst, Peter, 117
Hazratbal Mosque, 43–49, 135
Heir Apparent, 58, 96
Helvetic Republic (1798–1803), 86
Henderson, Arthur, 173
Herath, 40. See also Shivaratri
Hinayana, 6
The Hindu, 54
Historicity, 5, 14,
A History of Kashmir, 17
Hizbul Mujahideen, 135, 176
HMS Inn, 44
Hussain, Altaf, 72

Ibrahim, Sardar, 168
The Idea of Pakistan, 127
Ideological differences, 84
Ikhwanul Muslimeen, 135
Imtiaz, N., 164
India, Pakistan and the Secret Jihad, 57
Indian Air Force personnel, killings of, 134
Indian Military Academy (IMA), 67
Indian National Congress, 90, 129, 133
Indira–Sheikh Accord (1975), 92–93, 101, 107–08, 111–113. *See also* Delhi Agreement
Indo–China War (1962), 43, 66
Indo–Kashmir relations, 106
Indo–Pak War, 52, 66, 127
Indo–Pakistan problem, 52
Indo–Soviet Treaty of Peace, Friendship and Cooperation, 115
Indus Water Treaty, 73
'Informal war', 154
Instrument of Accession (1947), 92, 168–169, 188,
Inter-clan conflicts, 23
Intervention areas, 191
Invest Potential Index (N–SIPI), 161
Iqbal, Mohammad, 36–39, 41
Iran–Pakistan–India (IPI) gas pipeline, 90, 164
Islamic insurgency, 127

Jagmohan, appointment as governor, 132–33
Jahangir, 23, 199
Jammat–e–Islami, 176
Jammu and Kashmir Armed Police (JKAP), 133
Jammu and Kashmir Liberation Group (JKLF), 129–30, 134
Jammu and Kashmir Water Regulatory Authority, 157
Jarry, Ian, 67
Jha, Prem Shankar, 57

Jhelum, 3, 11, 74, 129, 148, 157, 172, 189, 197
Jihad, five phases of, 154–55
Jinnah, Mohammad Ali, 37–41, 83, 97–98, 100, 167
Joshi, Manoj, 126, 133

Kabali tribal raiders, 97, 180
Kah–naether ceremony, 129
Kak, Ram Chand, 167
Kak, Subhash, 15, 158
Kalhana, 14, 17, 20
Kamaraj Plan, 43
Karachi Gymkhana, 72, 75
Kargil conflict, 145
Kashir: Being a History of Kashmir, 35
Kashmir 1947: Rival Versions of History, 57
Kashmir 1947–1965: A Story Retold, 57
Kashmir and its People, 15
Kashmir conflict, 14, 154, 156
The Kashmir Conflict: From Empire to the Cold War (1945–66), 56
The Kashmir Dispute: 1947–2012, 56, 180
Kashmir of Europe. *See* Switzerland
Kashmir: The Vajpayee Years, 28, 54
Kashmir's accession to Pakistan, 98, 102, 167, 170–72, 176
Kashmiri Conference, 37
Kashmiri Lyrics, 11
Kashmiri nationalism, 176
Kashmiri Pandits, 3, 9–10, 22, 35, 58, 106, 110, 132, 134, 137–38, 140–42, 177, 197, 202–04
    demanding a homeland through Panun Kashmir, 177
    exodus of, 22, 110–11, 125, 132, 137, 142, 201–03
    killings of, 132, 134, 138, 203
    persecution of, 140
    return of the, 141–42
Kashmiri sentiments, 108
Kashmiri Shaivism, 5–13, 15, 18–19
    follower of, 8

philosophy of, 18–19
Kashmiris vs. Non–Kashmiris, 33–34
Kashmiriyat, 5, 8–9, 22, 58, 84, 88, 91,
    143, 156–57, 166–67, 177, 179, 198,
    208, 212
Kashyapa Mir, 15
Kashyap–pur (Kashyapmar), 15
Kasuri, Khurshid Mahmud, 145, 196
Kaul, Aditya Raj, 33
Kaul, Dattatreya, 35
Kaul, J.L., 11
Kaul, Ragho Ram, 35
Kaul, T.N., 115
Kaura, Vinay, 154
Kedourie, Elie, 175
Khan, Aslam, 39
Khan, Azam. *See* Afghan rule
Khanday, Mohammad Iqbal, 68
Khattak, Aslam Khan, 39
Khera, H.L., kidnapping of, 135
Khurshid, Salman, 89
Khusrau, Amir, 26
Khwaja Nur–ud–Din Eshai, 45
Kidnapping
    Doraiswamy, K., 135
    H.L. Khera, 135
    Rubaiya Sayeed, 135
King Harsha, 20
King Lalitaditya, 19, 25, 178
Kochak, Ghulam Nabi, 112
Koithara, Verghese, 73

Lahore Summit (1999), 144, 145
Lakshmanjoo, Swami, 13
Lal Ded, xvi, 4, 6, 89, 10, 35
    spiritual vision, 8
    strong critic of idolatry, 8
Lal Vaakh, 6,8, 9, 35, 142
Lalitaditya, 19, 25, 178
Lamb, Alastair, 166
*Languages of Belonging: Islam, Regional
    Identity, and the Making of Kashmir,*
    58

Lashkar-e-Taiba, 135
Lawrence, Walter, 28, 148
LeLaMOKSHI, 11, 166, 177, 190, 195,
    198, 199
Life expectancy, 160
Line of Actual Control (LoC), 116, 119,
    196
Lohar Chak, 23
Lone, Zaffar, 88
The Lost Rebellion: Kashmir in the Nineties,
    56, 126

Mahayana, 6, 18
Malik, Yasin, 130
Management tools, xi, xvi, 185–196
Marwah, Ved, 133
Menon, V.P., 168
Militancy, earlier phases of, 125-127,
    153-156
Mishra, Brijesh, 145
Mishra, R.K., 144, 145
Mohi-ud-Din Sufi, 35
Moi-e-Muqqadas, 44, 47
Mookerjee, Chittatosh, 106
Mountain Brigade, 48
Mountbatten, Lord, 56, 98, 102, 169
Mughal Gardens, 23
Muhajir Qaumi Movement (MQM), 73
Muhajirs, 73
'Mujahid Manzil', public meeting, 106
Mukherjee, Shyama Prasad, 103, 194
Multi-track diplomacy, 186
Mumbai attacks (2008), 78
Musharraf, General, 80. 90, 145, 146, 196
    four-point formula, 196
Mushir-ul-Haq, 135, 197
Muslim League, 37-39, 167
*My Life Years at the Bar, Bench and in
    Kashmir Politics,* 163

Naik, Amin, 68
Naik, Ghulam Nabi, 112, 131
Naik, Niaz A., 144

Naipaul, V.S., 29
Namsa Devi, Indrakshi, 44
Nand Rishi, 8, 135, 143
Napoleon, 86
Nash Equilibrium, 179, 180, 185, 187, 199
Nash, John, 185
National Conference, 40, 43, 49, 97, 102,
    104, 108, 117, 126, 130, 133, 194
National Council of Applied Economic
    Research (NCAER), 161
National Defence Academy (NDA), 66
National Institute of Technology (NIT), 44
National Security Council (NSC), 124
Nationalism, 175-177
Nayar, Kuldip, 173
Nehru, Jawaharlal, 11, 16, 43, 47, 52, 108,
    110, 198Nehru, Motilal Kaul, 110
Neither a Hawk Nor a Dove, 145, 196
New York Times, 118
Nilamata Purana, 14, 16
Nishaandehs, 45
Nishat Bagh, 45
Noor Jehan, 23
Noor Khan, Air Marshal, 53
Noorani, A.G., 56, 180
Nooruddin, Sheikh, 7, 135. *See also* Nund
    Rishi
Nund Rishi, 135, 143, 198
Nutrition-related indicators, 160

Observer Research Foundation (ORF), x,
    xii, 144, 210
Oil & Gas Conference (2007), 77
Operation Gibraltar, 52, 53

Pakistan and the Sacred Jihad, 51
Pakistan Army, Islamization of, 83, 128, 129
    Zia-ul-Haq's tenure, 128
Pakistan Military Academy (PMA), 127
Pakistan Occupied Kashmir (PoK), 104,
    118, 130, 134, 147,148, 156, 159, 170,
    179, 187, 190, 192
Pakistan's irredenta, 83

Pandita, Rahul, 58
Pant, Govind Ballabh, 104
Parekh, Deepak, 163
Pareto optimality, 125, 185, 187, 198, 199
Pari Mahal, 23
Parry, John, 71
Parthasarathy, G., 91, 107, 119
Patel, Sardar, 99, 107
Peace pipeline. *See* Iran-Pakistan-India
    (IPI) gas pipeline
People's Democratic Party (PDP), 194
People's war, 127
Petroleum Institute of Pakistan, 77
Pir Giasuddin, 109
Pir Maqbool Gilani, 53
Political and bureaucratic commitment,
    162
'Politicization of ethno-national'
    communities, 176
Polling percentage, 33
Pramanik, Surapati, 185
Praveen Swami, 52, 57
Princely states, 96, 99, 100, 167
Prisoner's Dilemma (PD), 186
Prisoners of war (POWs), 116
Protestants and Catholics, civil war, 87
Proxy votes, 109
Proxy war, 127
Psychiatric illnesses, 164
Psycho-social distrurbances, 164
Puranic geography, 15

Qasim, Mir, 46, 50, 108, 109, 163
Qasim, Mohammad Bin, 20
Qazi, Manzoor, 211
Queen Didda (AD 981–1003), 20
Quit Kashmir movement, 53

Radcliffe Commission, 171, 173
Radcliffe, Cyril, 99, 173
Radha Kumar, 112
Radical Islam, 81, 82, 157
Radio Azad Kashmir, 147, 148

Radio Kashmir, 47, 147
Rajatarangini, 14, 17, 20, 41, 50
Raliv, Tsaliv, Galiv, 137
Ramgardhia, 81
Rampur, Nawab of, 66, 67
Ranjit Singh, 24, 139, 140
Rao, K.V. Krishna, 54
Rao, P.V. Narasimha, 54, 198
Rasool, Ghulam, 35, 129-131
Razdan, Nidhi, 33
Reimagining Pakistan, 57
Reliance Industries Ltd., 77
Religious tolerance, 3
Renan, Ernest, 175
Retallack, David, 71
Rinchan (Buddhist prince), 20, 21
Rishi Nuruddin, 8
Rising Kashmir, 197
Roy, Tapan Kumar, 185
Rumi, poetry and philosophy of, 37
Rumour-mongering, 148
Rural vs. urban poverty ratio, 160

Sadhu, Sanjay, 88
Sadiq, G.M., 46, 50, 53, 115
Sainik School, Ghorakhal (SSGK), 65–67
Sapru, Tej Bahadur, 96
Satisar, 14–15
Satyagraha-type movement, 142
Saudi Arabia, Islam in, 88-90
Saudi Arabian General Investment
    Authority (SAGIA), 70
Saxena, J.N., 133
Sayeed, Mufti Mohammad, 135
Sayeed, Rubaiya, 135
'Scientific humanism', 19, 165
Second-class citizens. *See* Muhajirs
Sen, Amartya, 150, 159
Service Selection Board (SSB), 67
Services and economic activities, 173
Shah Mir, 5, 20-22, 137, 155, 201
Shah, Ghulam Mohammad, 53, 112
Shah, Sadruddin, 21

Shah, Yousuf, 22, 23
Shahi, Chashma, 23
Shaivism and Sufism, congruence
    between, 9
Shalimar Garden, 23
Shamsuddin, Sultan, 21
Sharif, Nawaz, xiv, 57, 72, 144, 145
Sheikh-Indira Accord (1975), 101
Sherwani, Maqbool, 180
Shias, 23, 74
Shivaratri, 39, 40
Sikandar, Sultan, 21
Sikh rule, 24
Sikh separatists, 127
Silk Route, 163
Simla Accord, 114, 125, 126
Simla Agreement (1972), 92, 106, 115, 119,
    120, 187
Simla Conference, 115-119
Singh, Amrit Pal, 208, 211
Singh, Gobinder, 133
Singh, J.P., 68
Singh, Karan, 46-49, 58, 92, 96, 102
Singh, Khushwant, 36
Singh, Manmohan, 78, 146
Singh, Pratap, 93, 174
Sir Creek boundary issue, 145
Social media, xvi, 33, 148–154
    and Perceptions, 149–154
    Facebook accounts, 153
    young militants, 153
Spiritual tradition, 4
A Spy for All Seasons, 52
'Standstill agreement', 167, 173
State stood, fiscal liabilities of, 162
State subject of J&K, 71
Stein, Aurel, 148
Stein, M.A., 17
Sterba, James P., 94, 118
Sufi Islam, 10, 88, 156
Sufism, xi, xv, 5, 7, 9, 165-167, 179
Sunnis, 74
Switzerland, 85-8872-74

early history of, 86
melting pot of distinct cultures, 86
permanent armed neutrality status, 86
Synergic culture, 8, 143, 165, 177, 198, 207

Taploo, Tika Lal, 132
Tashkent Conference, 116
Tata Institute of Fundamental Research
    (TIFR), 16
Tata, Ratan, 163
The Telegraph, 36
Teng, Yusuf Mohammad, 130
Territorial nationalism, 176
Thakur, D.D., 111, 163
The Times, 100, 170
The Times of India, 105
Transparency and meritocracy in
    employment, 157
Trika philosophy, 7, 19. *See also* Kashmiri
    Shaivism
'Truth machine', 27, 32
Two-nation theory, 36-40, 97, 100,
    102, 167, 171. *See also* Jinnah,
    Mohammad Ali

UN Drug Control Programme (UNDCP),
    164
UN Human Rights Convention, 89
*An Uncertain Glory—India and its
    Contradictions*, 159
United Progressive Alliance (UPA), 112

Universal divinity, 9, 36
Urban vs. rural divide, 156
Uttarakhand, creation of, 69

Vajpayee, Atal Bihari, xi, 144-146, 198
    Geneva visit, 89
    The Valley of Kashmir, 28, 343
Vairocana (first Kashmiri missionary), 18
Voter turnout, 160

Wadi Ki Awaz (radio programme), 147
Wahhabism, 88
Wakhlu, Somnath, 92
Wani, Burhan, 148, 153, 154
Wani, Farooq, 129, 131, 211
War and Diplomacy in Kashmir, 56
Wazwan, 33, 40, 78, 131
Wheeler, General, 66

Zaidi, Akhtar, 70
Zain-ul-Abidin, 22, 23, 139, 148, 179, 197,
    201
Zardari, Asif Ali, 78
Zargar, Abdul Ghani, 135
Zia-ul-Haq, 83, 100, 127, 128
    'Islamic' orientation of the army, 128
    Islamization step, 128
    marginalized American influence, 128
Zulju, 20
Zutshi, Chitralekha, 58, 202